ENGAGING • RESPONDING • REFLECTING

EfM

An EfM Publication, the Beecken Center, Sewanee, Tennessee
ISBN: 979-8-218-68173-9

Designer: Hannah Kunz; Contributing writers: Joshua D. Booher, Rick Brewer, Angela Hock-Brewer, Kevin M. Goodman, Elizabeth Lang, Karen Meridith, Kay McCall, Leah Romanelli De Jesus, Maggie Taliaferro, and Sissie Wile.

EfM:
JOURNAL

Education for Ministry

TABLE OF CONTENTS

ABOUT EDUCATION FOR MINISTRY

Education for Ministry began in 1975 at the School of Theology of The University of the South in Sewanee, Tennessee. Throughout its 50-year history, participants have engaged in spiritual study and reflection that has deeply enriched their lives. Many people think that one must be ordained in order to be a "minister," but a Christian's vows at baptism and confirmation state that all baptized Christians are called to be ministers. God calls all of us to be active participants in the whole ministry of the Church. The EfM program is designed to help Christian people prepare for their ministry. EfM helps people develop an understanding of their faith through the study of Scripture, church history, and theology, and by bringing that material into dialogue with the events of their everyday life.

EfM's Contemplative Journal was created as a personal companion to your seminar work. If you are continuing your EfM journey, you have already experienced the way this program weaves multiple strands into a rich tapestry of experience. Throughout your time in EfM, you will hear from a variety of voices—from both outside and within EfM. Some of these voices may be familiar, and others may be new. All of them engage you in a dialogue with God that began thousands of years ago. Whether something speaks to you from the past to inform you of how we got here, lives in the present trying to make sense of the world today, or foretells of a future closer to the Kingdom of God, they are all important perspectives to be heard.

If you are new to EfM, you will be introduced to a variety of spiritual practices, voices, and perspectives:

- Our core texts provide the voice of vetted scholarship.
- Our Common Lessons introduce you to different spiritual perspectives geared to the theme of the year.
- The Pathwright online syllabus leads you into practices that enhance your ability to reflect on your experiences.

EfM is a program delivered by a community of diverse mentors, through online and onsite groups. Each mentor brings a unique perspective to the program as they guide their group through conversation with God and each other. Mentors have the freedom to creatively deliver the content of the program within the structure of the program. No two seminar experiences are alike—some groups consist of members within a single parish, others span the globe in an online format. Each experience is colored by the different voices of the participants and how the mentor weaves the voices of the program and the participants together.

HOW TO USE THE EfM: JOURNAL

This journal is designed to be used with all EfM formation products, including EfM: Classic, EfM: Wide Angle, EfM: Reflections, EfM: Pilgrimage, and EfM: Catechumenate. The pages are designed to capture journal reflections, theological reflections, and insights from seminars, as well as their implications.

The journal invites creativity and inspires focus. There is space to respond to journal prompts, make notes about Engage sources, and track Theological Reflections through the four sources and four movements. There is even an area just to doodle. The possibilities are limitless. You can capture prayer concerns and thanksgivings, note "Position" and "Apply" statements, react to a reading, save thoughts and feelings, draw images and mind maps, record metaphors, engage moments from scripture and the history of the Church, and write down a resource shared in the seminar.

Throughout the journal, there are short essays about EfM's Core Practices and other articles to support and inspire all on their journey of faith.

At the back of the journal are sets of "Stepping Stones," a workspace for you to track the movements of your spiritual autobiography and plan what you are comfortable sharing with your group.

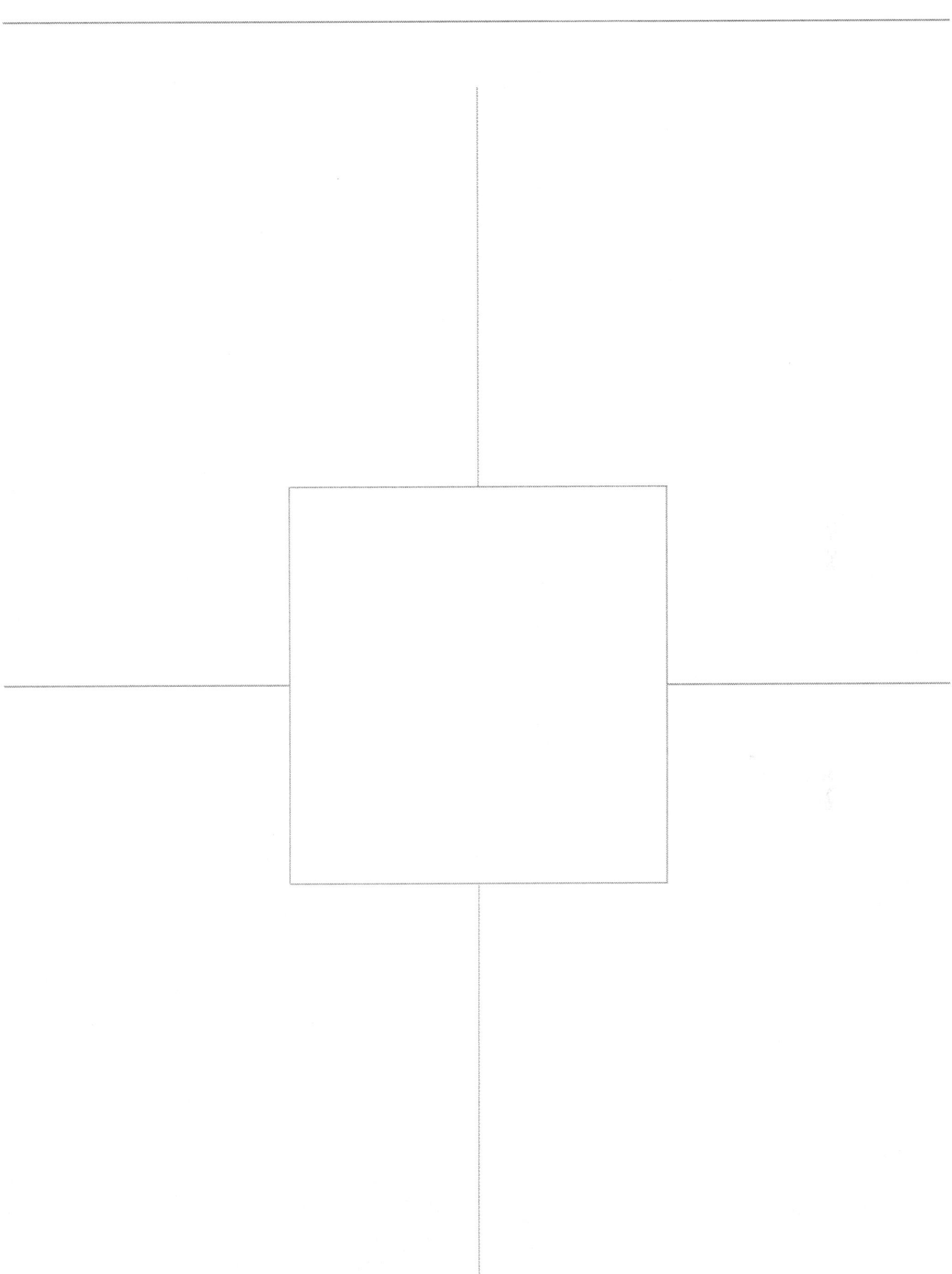

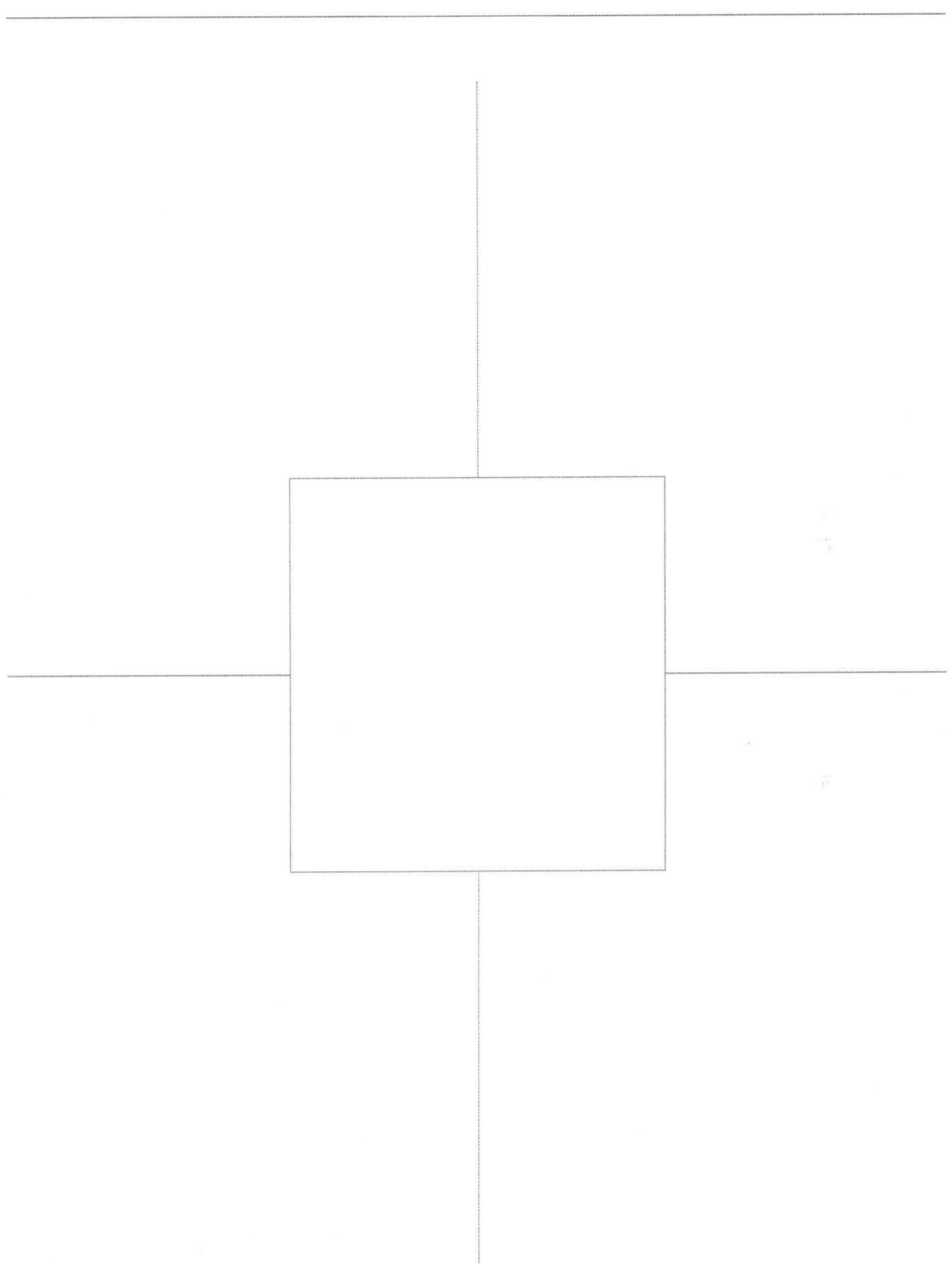

CORE PRACTICES

EfM invites us to practice the best things about spiritual community: diverse people in earnest and honest conversation as we make meaning of the world and care for each other as individuals. The lessons we learn from each other and the people with whom we grow stay with us forever. Many of us yearn for safe places to learn, to discover meaning, and to wonder about God. These five core practices guide all EfM constituents in creating and maintaining small, trusted communities where authentic seeking and interaction thrive.

Living in Community

Where can we find friends with whom we can honestly be ourselves with all our questions and all our doubts? Intentional small groups maintain spaces in which we can face issues, lament losses, celebrate joys, and share dreams. We do this through a structure of:

- Sharing themed autobiographies
- Listening with empathetic respect
- Setting expectations that ensure the group is trustworthy

Prayer and Worship

Why do we need to worship? What does it look like to worship with friends without the structure of a Sunday service? Whether we are lifelong Episcopalians or spiritual in a way that exceeds definition, we all
need rituals that mark what matters and connect us with God. Together we employ words, art, music, movement, and/or silence in prayer. This practice:

- Opens awareness of the mysterious
- Reveals the wonderful which is beyond us and within us
- Connects us with the Divine and one another

Theological Reflection

We hear that "God is everywhere" but how do we learn to pay attention to our experiences so that the Divine becomes more evident? What do we do with the disconnect between our beliefs and behaviors? How and where does Christian faith and tradition intersect with culture? Theological reflection is a guided discussion which brings diverse sources of knowledge into conversation. It addresses theological questions and categories such as wholeness/goodness, brokenness/alienation, recognition/awareness, reorientation/repentance, and restoration/redemption. Theological reflection unites:

- The emotional with the intellectual
- The theoretical with the practical
- The analytical with the poetic

When we apply it to our lives, this process helps us live with integrity and wisdom. It helps us embody the interconnectedness of our faith, bodies, culture, and context so that we live as whole people.

Study of Christian Tradition

What are our questions about God? What do we wonder about Jesus? How has the Church developed over the years? Have our ideas about faith changed and, if so, what do we do about it? Discovering an informed, mature comprehension of Christian tradition includes:

- Studying the Bible using contemporary scholarship that employs historical, literary, and theological criticisms
- Learning about the evolution of Christianity from its Jewish origins until today
- Studying ethics, theologians' perspectives—ancient and modern, foundational doctrines like the Trinity and the Incarnation, and exploring intersections with other faiths

Vocational Discernment

How do we find and create meaning? What does it look like to integrate faith into daily life? Vocational discernment is the companion and result of the other core practices. It is not merely identifying a job or a task.

- It is discovering "who we are becoming" individually and as a group.
- It affects how we relate to others and respond to opportunities.
- Vocational discernment is akin to love because it is characterized by a deep sense of desire, commitment, joy, and freedom.

Ministry involves "doing." It also involves "being." It is being present and standing with a person in crisis and being a person of compassion. Ministry involves many things. Here are some examples:

- It is listening to another's story
- It is caring for the young and old
- It is working for justice
- It is seeking to create a good environment for those who are seeking a better world
- It is maintaining a home
- It is receiving expressions of concern from others
- It is teaching someone to read
- It is feeding and clothing persons who need accompaniment

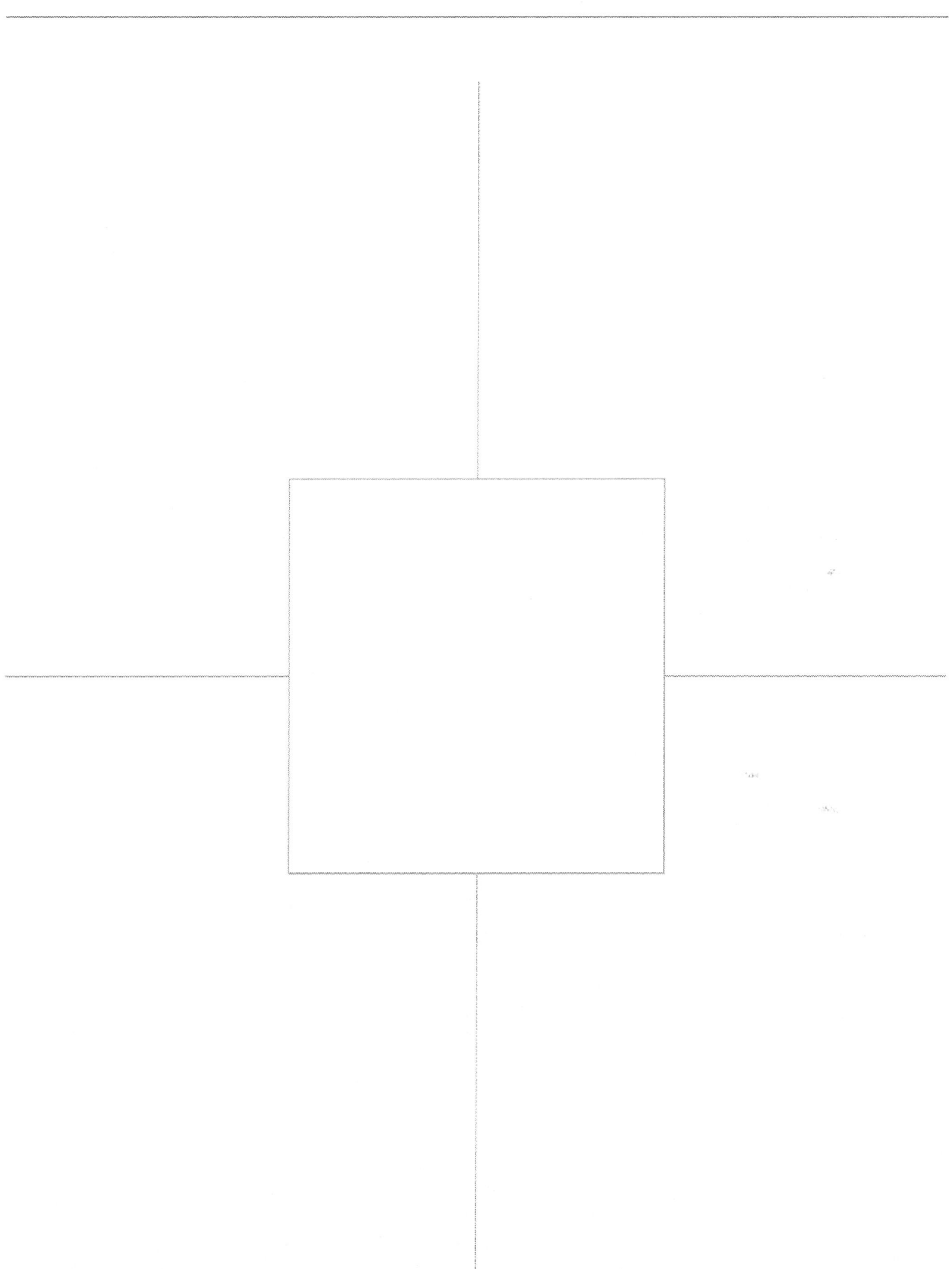

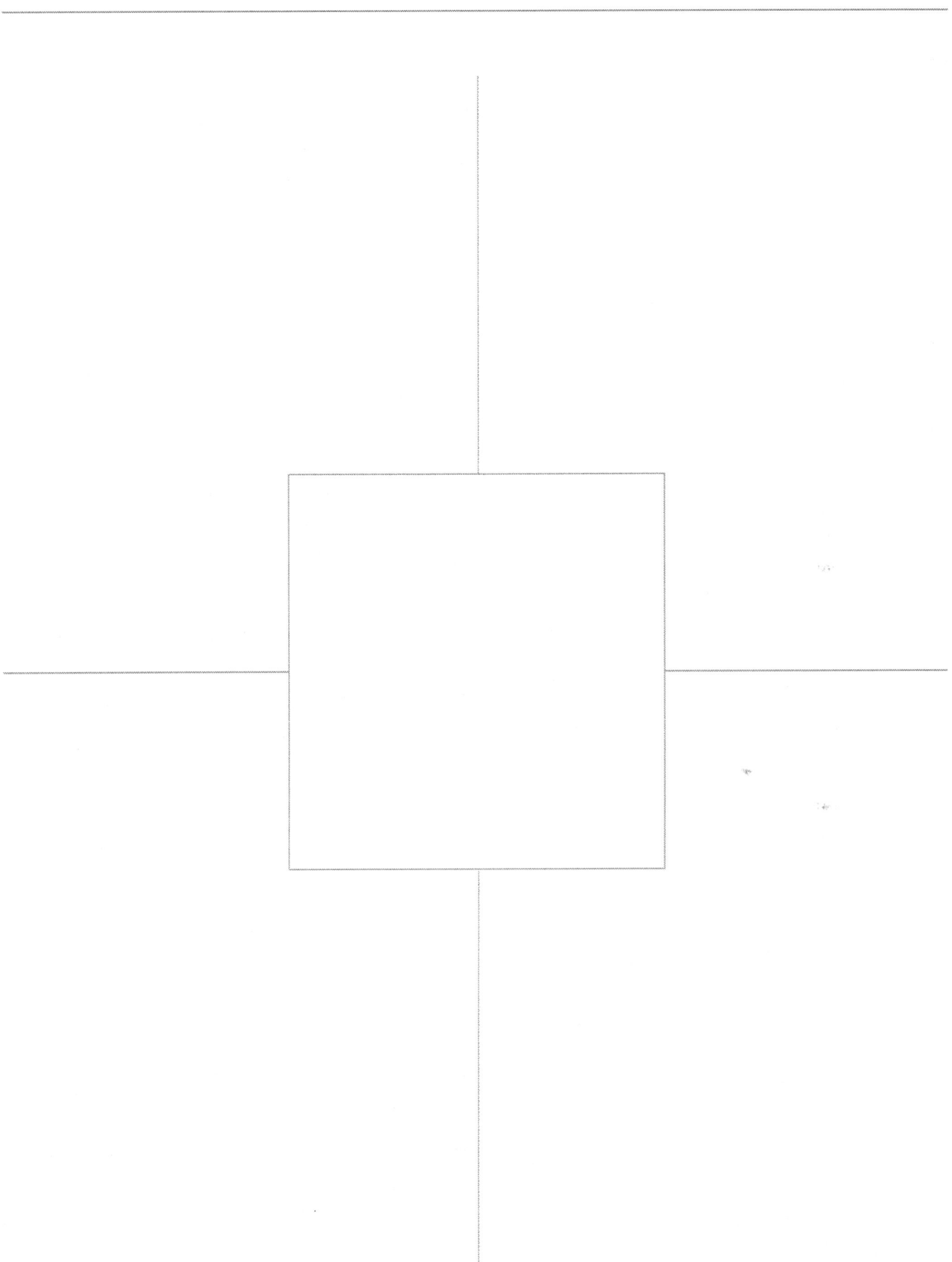

"I need a God who is bigger and more nimble and mysterious than what I could understand and contrive. Otherwise it can feel like I am worshipping nothing more than my own ability to understand the divine."

–Nadia Bolz-Weber
Pastrix: The Cranky, Beautiful Faith of a Sinner & Saint

SPIRITUALITY

The journey with God, striving for peace, justice, and compassion in Christian ministry can be challenging. Regular practice in the disciplines of prayer, worship, study, reflection, and service support us in this journey through an enlivened spirituality that nourishes our whole being. An enlivening spirituality fills our hearts with courage for resisting the injustice, hatred, disrespect, and violence that diminish or destroy created life. A healthy and sustaining spirituality anticipates new knowledge, welcomes the search for truth, and dares to live with uncertainty.

Spirituality is not only an individual matter. To be in Christ is to be a part of the whole body of Christ. We are members of a community of faith. Reflecting upon our common life with others can yield significant spiritual insight. Our spirituality reflects how we live with others.

The human journey becomes a God journey once one is touched by truth, or beauty, or love, that can be neither explained or discounted. The power of the wondrous overwhelms, and one is propelled into deepening the knowing and loving that overflow into passion to declare this Wholly Other presence and share the experience with others. The spiritual journey involves living within an awareness of God, God's creation, and God's people.

Answers to fundamental existential questions morph into different shapes as one travels through life, as changing circumstances bring again to the surface questions that earlier were put to rest. Identity builds on a career, marriage, family, acquisitions, and accomplishments require radical adjustments over time. When the job ends, people die, marriages fail, belongings deteriorate, or accomplishments fade, the questions of identity and purpose resume. "Who am I?" and "Who am I becoming?" reappear.

As we encounter and respond to life's fragmentation and isolation, how is God involved in creating, redeeming, and sanctifying wholeness? A practical, integrated approach to attending to one's spiritual beliefs and actions holds the potential to awaken practicing God-seekers to unity and wholeness. For Christians, striving for wholeness and holiness is an ongoing process of integration that invites contemporary knowledge into dialogue with Christian heritage, seeking to reconcile individual disconnections between belief and behavior.

St. Augustine of Hippo prayed, "...because you have made us and drawn us to yourself, our heart is unquiet until it rests in you." Our spiritual journey opens us to new and ever renewed paths that deepen love of self, others, creation, and God. From birth, each person heads into the future in hope of finding paths of beauty, goodness, and truth. Cherishing beauty, doing good, knowing truth, and worshipping holiness reinforce one's spiritual journey. Along the way, the search for belonging, intimacy, contributing, and eternity are indications of desiring the divine-human communion.

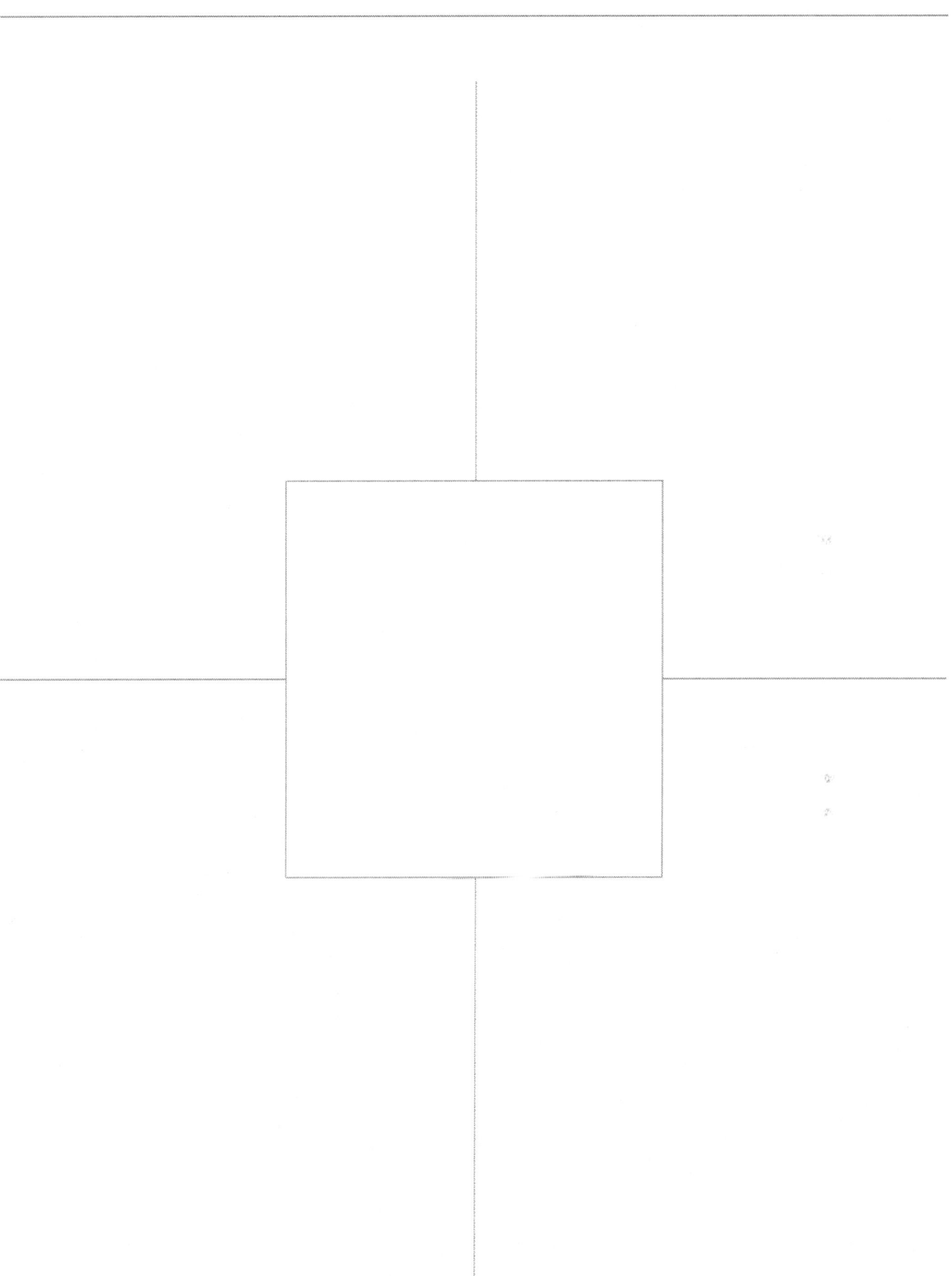

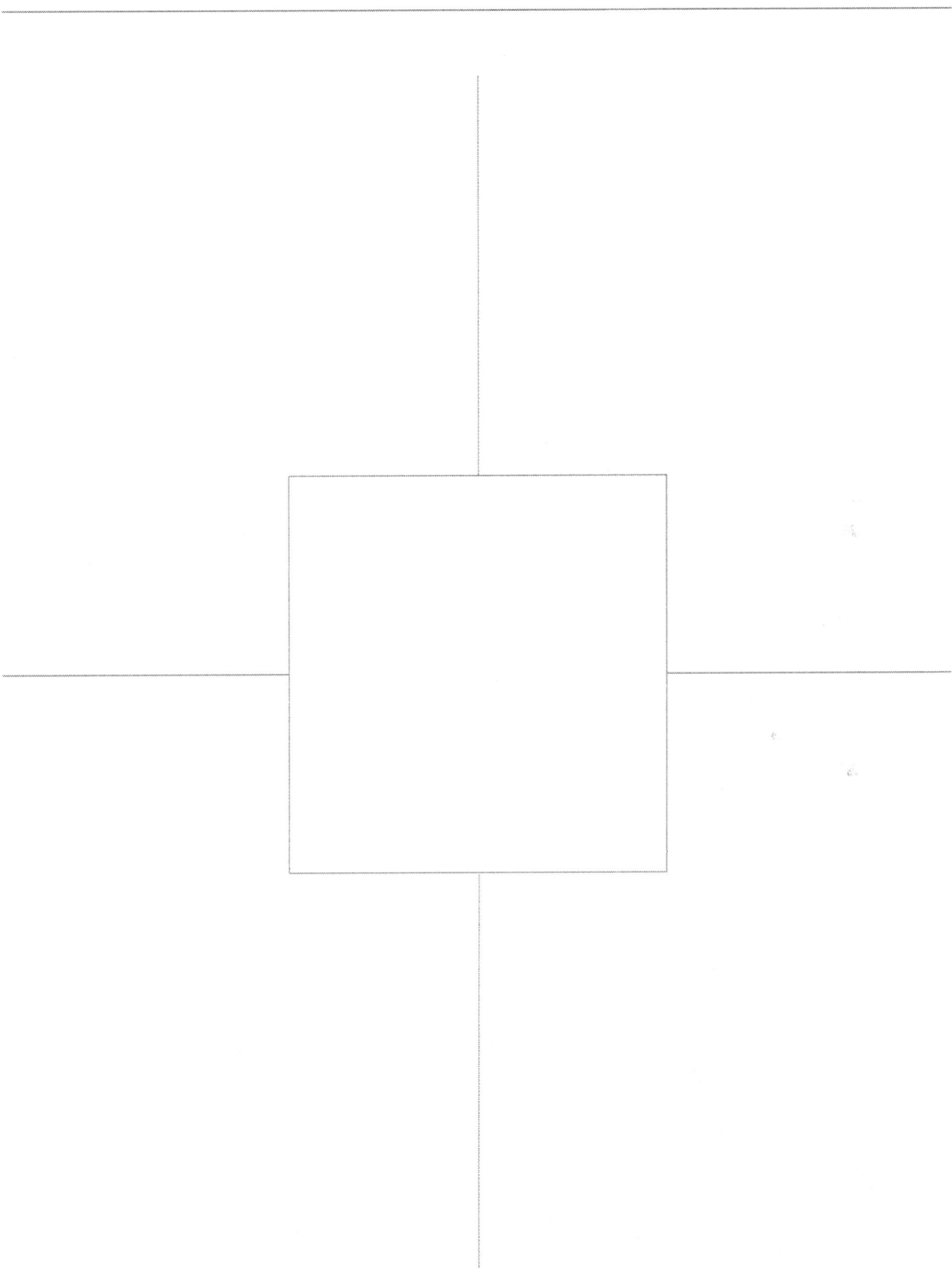

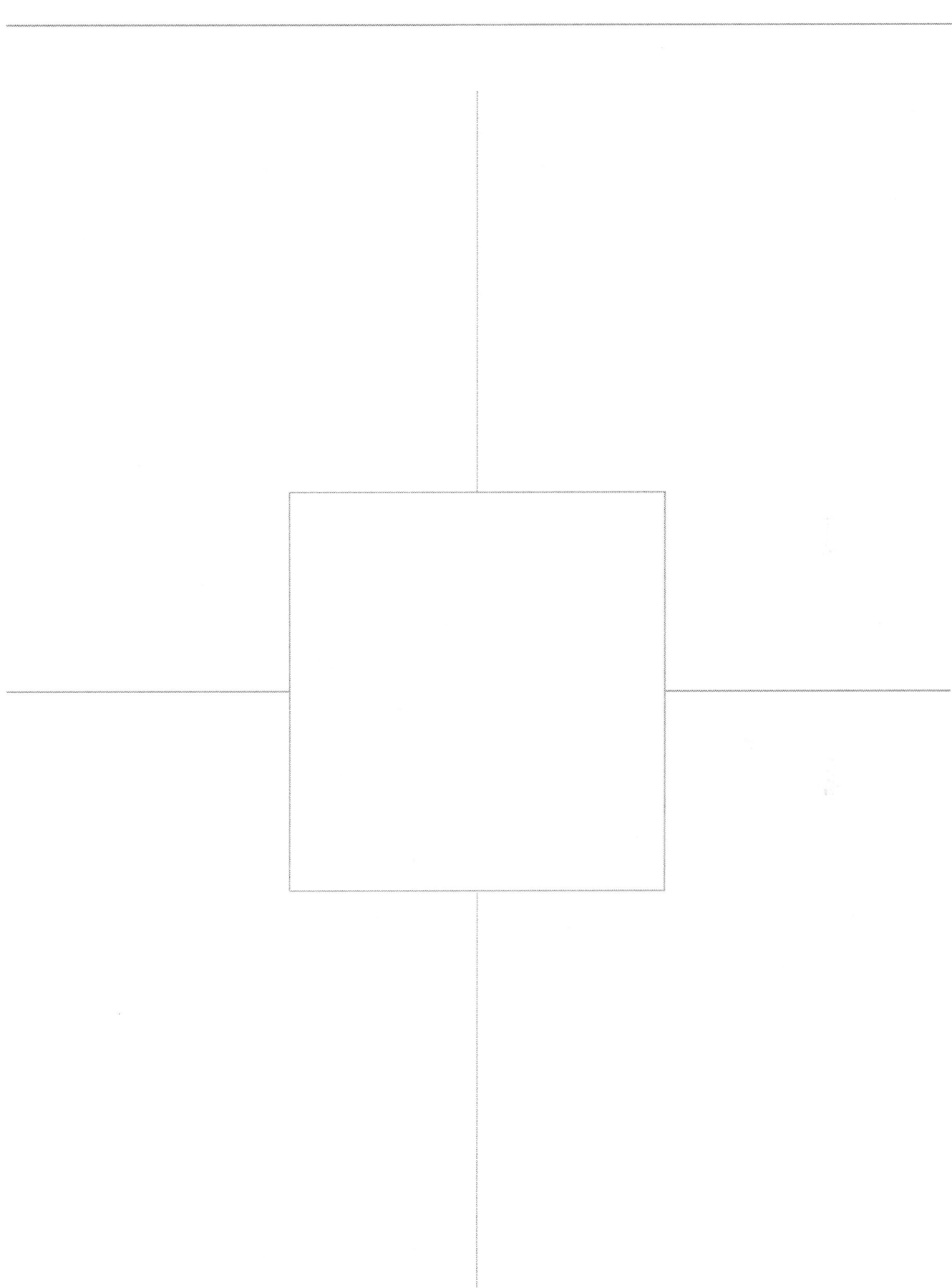

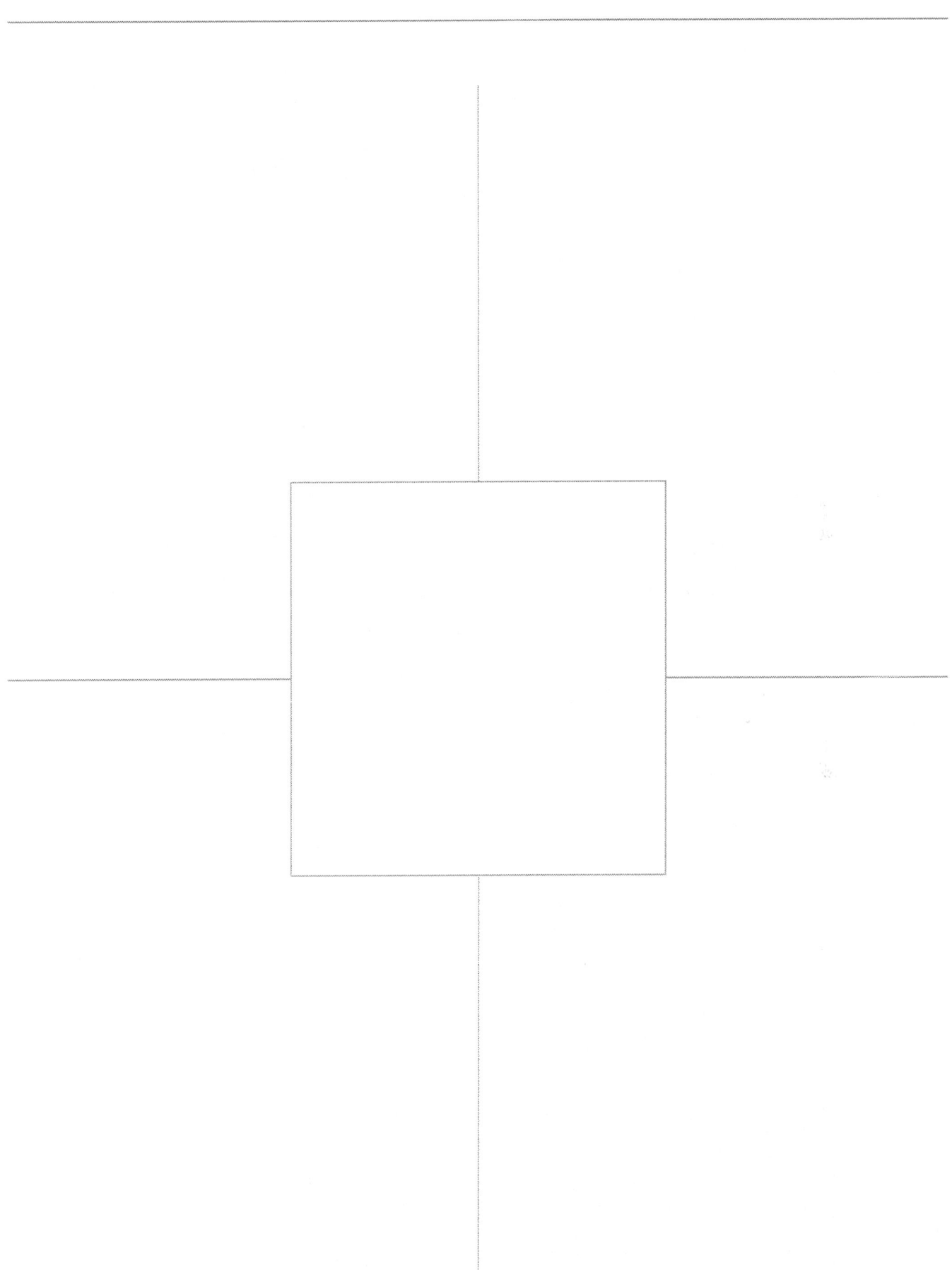

"Without the power of imagination, we cannot envision a different past, present, and future... What we cannot imagine, we cannot live into and struggle for."

–Kwok Pui-lan
Postcolonial Imagination and Feminist Theology

SPIRITUAL AUTOBIOGRAPHY

A spiritual autobiography is the story of significant events, people, and places that have influenced your relationship with God. It tells the story of how you have come to be the person you are and how you have come to hold your own beliefs. The sharing of autobiographies builds trust and understanding. It also provides an opportunity to discover the connections and themes within your personal story and thus gain new perspectives. The experience of hearing other life stories lets us know that we are not alone in God's world. Through our sharing with a group of people whom we can trust, we create communities of learning that support, and may also, challenge us.

Each year, EfM participants are asked to recall their life story through a different lens. We believe our experiences are the primary resource for theological education. Call, discernment, vocation, and ministry are embedded in our spiritual journeys. The process of telling and retelling our story helps those themes come more clearly into our consciousness.

Preparing a spiritual autobiography each year provides a way to deepen our understanding of both Christian life and ministry. By virtue of our baptism, we are called to ministry, guided and pushed by personal gifts, passions, skills, experiences, and interests.

Martin Buber, a 20th-century philosopher and Jewish theologian, is reputed to have said that he could never hold a significant conversation with another person until he had heard the other's life story. We need the experience of hearing other life stories to know that we are not alone in God's world. Sharing your spiritual autobiography is a way to say, "Here I am."

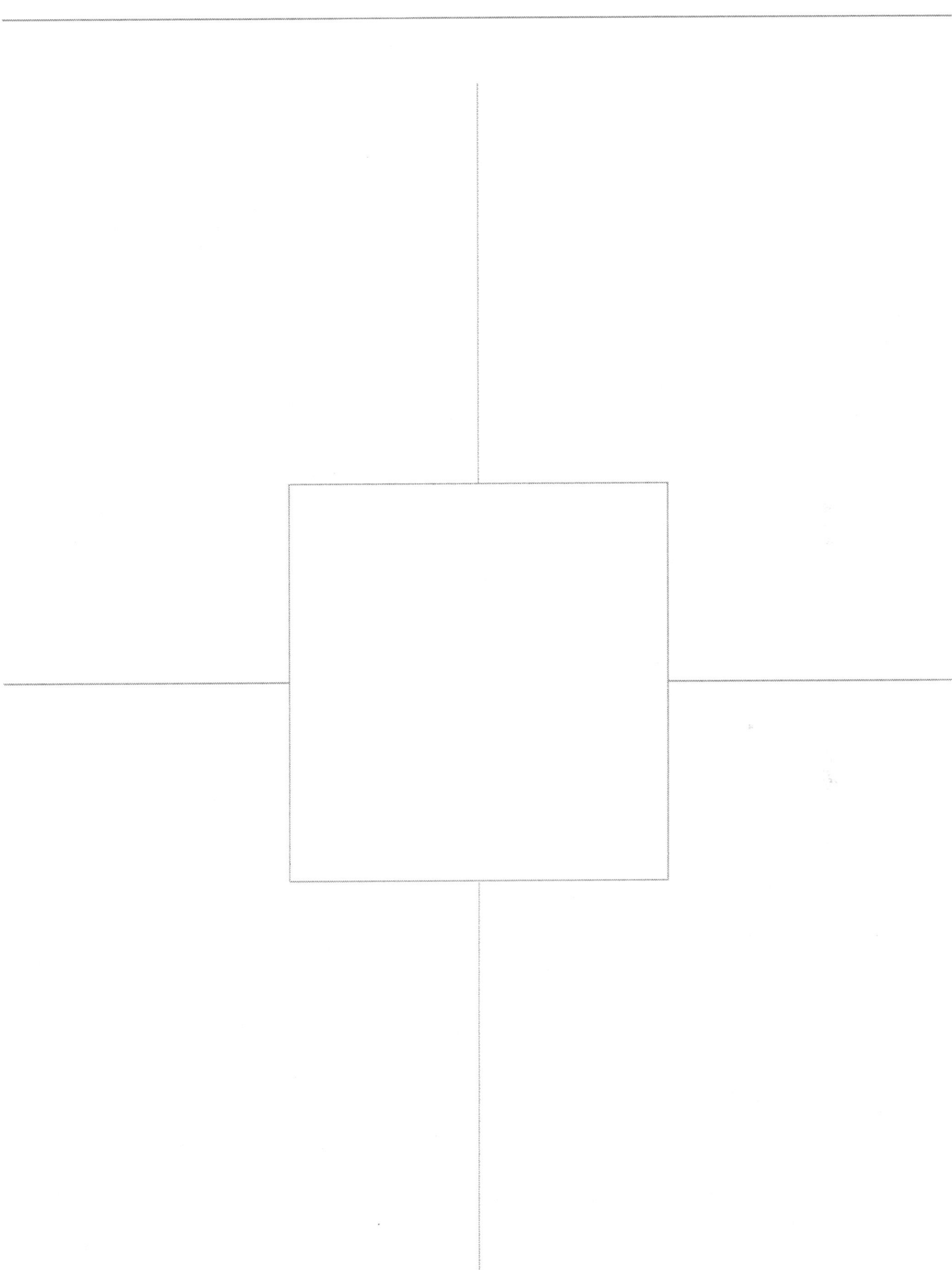

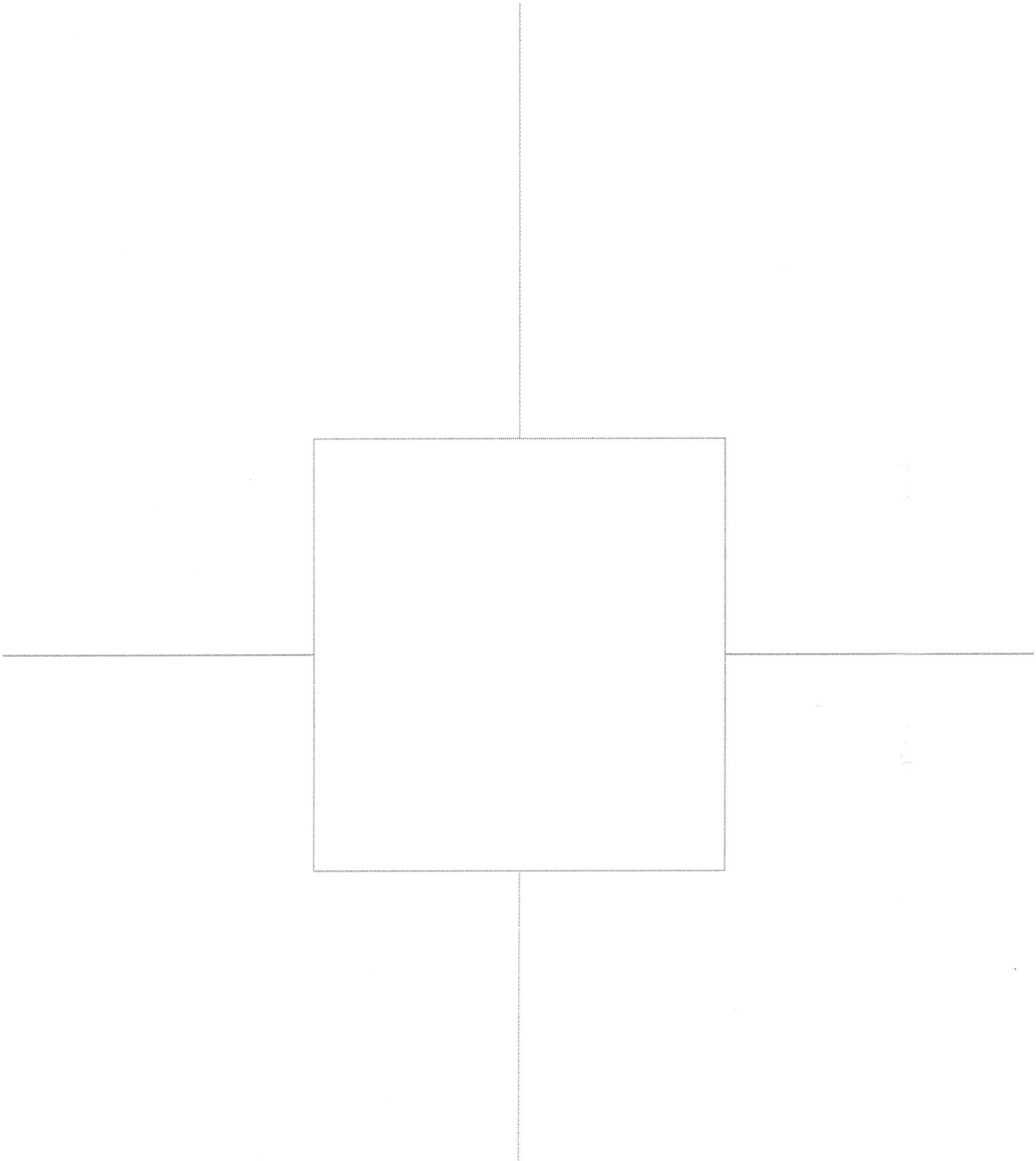

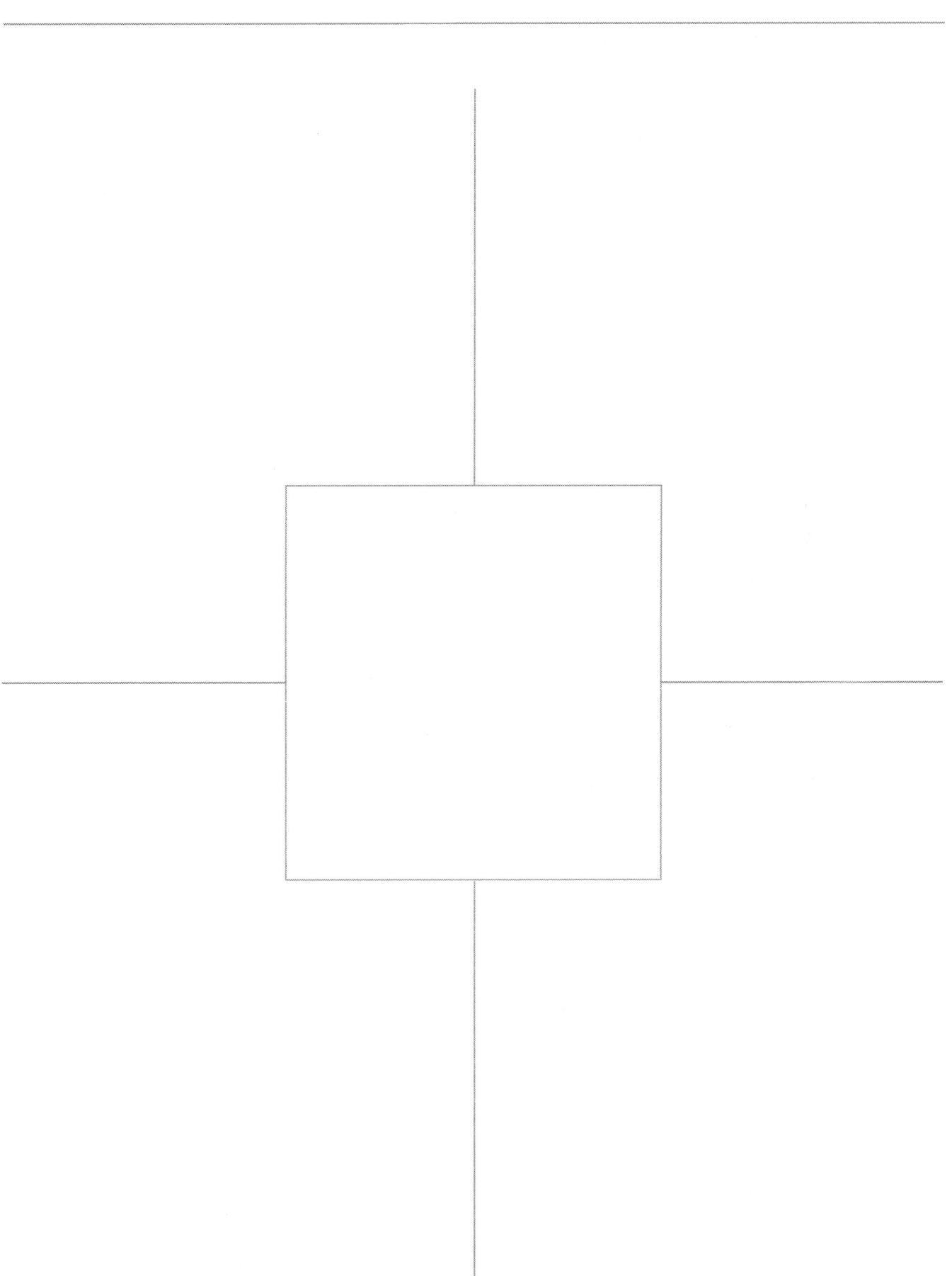

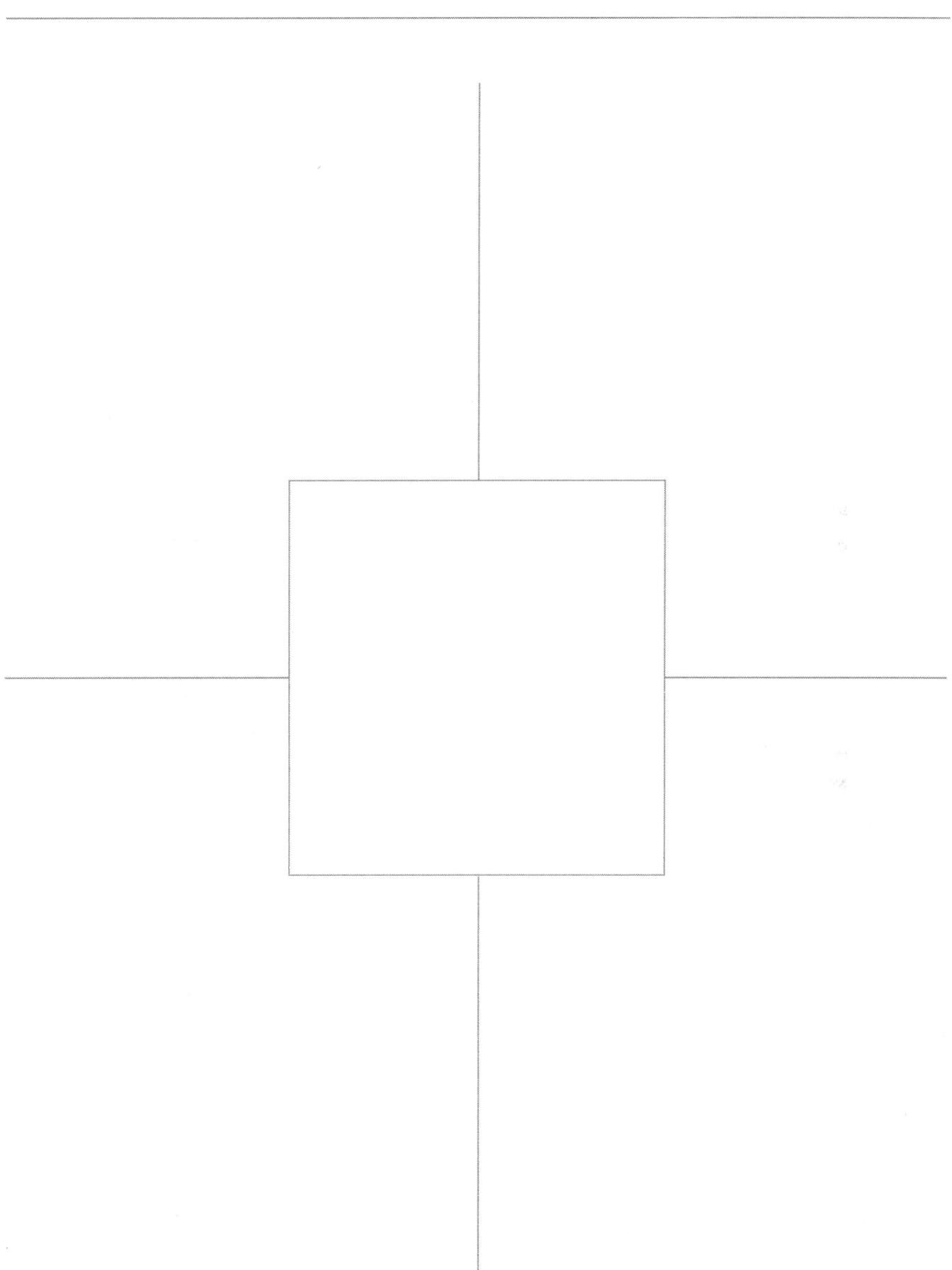

"Great art is not a matter of presenting one side or another, but presenting a picture so full of the contradictions, tragedies, and insights of the period that the impact is at once disturbing and satisfying."

–Pauli Murray
To Speak a Defiant Word: Sermons and Speeches on Justice and Transformation

THEOLOGICAL REFLECTION

Theological Reflection occurs naturally and spontaneously throughout the Church as committed people read the Bible, participate in worship, struggle to find meaning in the events of their lives, and discuss their beliefs, hopes, and fears.

Theological reflection is:

- a journey deeper into our experience and knowledge of God
- a disciplined method of exploring real world issues and contextualizing them within our faith and lives
- a conversation which opens us to "revelation" or new truth and meaning for living
- a set of tools that equips people for living their faith by enhancing their spiritual awareness and integrating belief and behavior

The Four Sources of Knowledge

In EfM there are four areas into which we categorize our collective knowledge. These four areas come from both internal and external sources:

1. Christian Tradition: (outside) scripture, doctrine, church history, liturgy and worship, church architecture, religious symbols, commentaries
2. Contemporary Culture: (outside) social norms, arts, sciences, the media, secular history, politics, economics, socio-cultural environment, secular symbols, work environments
3. Personal Experience: (inside) actions, behaviors, thoughts, feelings, experiences, fears and hopes
4. Personal Belief: (inside) positions, opinions, attitudes, convictions, hunches, perspectives

The EfM Method of Theological Reflection

1. **Identify** a focus. Start with something specific from any of the four sources and notice details, energy, and the tone of this initial piece.

   Example:

   (From PERSONAL EXPERIENCE) As I was driving, I saw a man at an intersection with a sign: "Need work & $$." I wondered what to do. I considered giving him cash but worried that I would be supporting his addiction. I thought of taking him home and paying him to weed my garden, but was uncomfortable with that. I wondered about telling him about agencies that could help him, but I knew little about them.

   The chosen focus was a man in need.

2. **Explore** the focus with theological perspective questions. Ask a few questions from categories such as wholeness/goodness, brokenness/alienation, recognition/awareness, reorientation/repentance, and restoration/redemption. One can ask about the nature of God or human nature.

   Example:

   What is broken/alienated? There are needy people; addiction is prevalent; some people are dangerous.

   Where is awareness/recognition? I do not know how to help him. I don't know much about local agencies that could help.

   Where is redemption? It might be recognizing the dignity of the man and treating him with respect. It might include becoming more informed about local agencies and supporting them.

3. **Connect** with the other three sources. Bring the other sources of knowledge into the conversation. Notice similarities and differences. The interchange among Christian tradition, cultural examples, personal experiences, and beliefs provokes new questions, insights, and answers. It shows people how faith matters.

   Example:

   CHRISTIAN TRADITION: The story of the blind beggar Bartimaeus and Jesus.

   Where is there brokenness? The crowd tells Bartimaeus to be quiet when he calls out to Jesus. What is redemptive? Jesus pays attention to Bartimaeus when others don't. He asks him what he wants, thus recognizing his dignity. Upon the beggar's request, Jesus heals him of his blindness.

   CONTEMPORARY CULTURE: Taylor Swift's song "Now That We Don't Talk." What is redemptive? The phrases "I don't have to pretend," and "the way back to my dignity" highlight self-respect and dignity.

   PERSONAL POSITION: What is redemptive? I think that people with needs deserve respect. I think everyone should be treated with dignity. I think self-respect is necessary.

4. **Apply** to daily life. This last step ensures that theological reflection goes beyond intellectual entertainment. The implication may include the need for further exploration and prayer and will be specific to each person's life. The application may integrate belief and behavior.

   Example:

   When I want to help someone, I will ask for permission and/or inquire about what they want or need. I will support selected agencies that help people obtain jobs.

   When people treat me badly, I will respect myself.

Through the EfM model of theological reflection done in community, people gain awareness of themselves and others and deeper knowledge of Christian teaching while they:

- Think critically
- Identify subtle ways they are influenced
- Converse rather than debate
- Move conversations toward insight and action
- Obtain knowledge of Christian tradition
- Integrate various sources of knowledge
- Better align what we believe with how we behave

As we practice the discipline of theological reflection we grow intellectually, spiritually, and personally and begin to recognize the extraordinary in the ordinary.

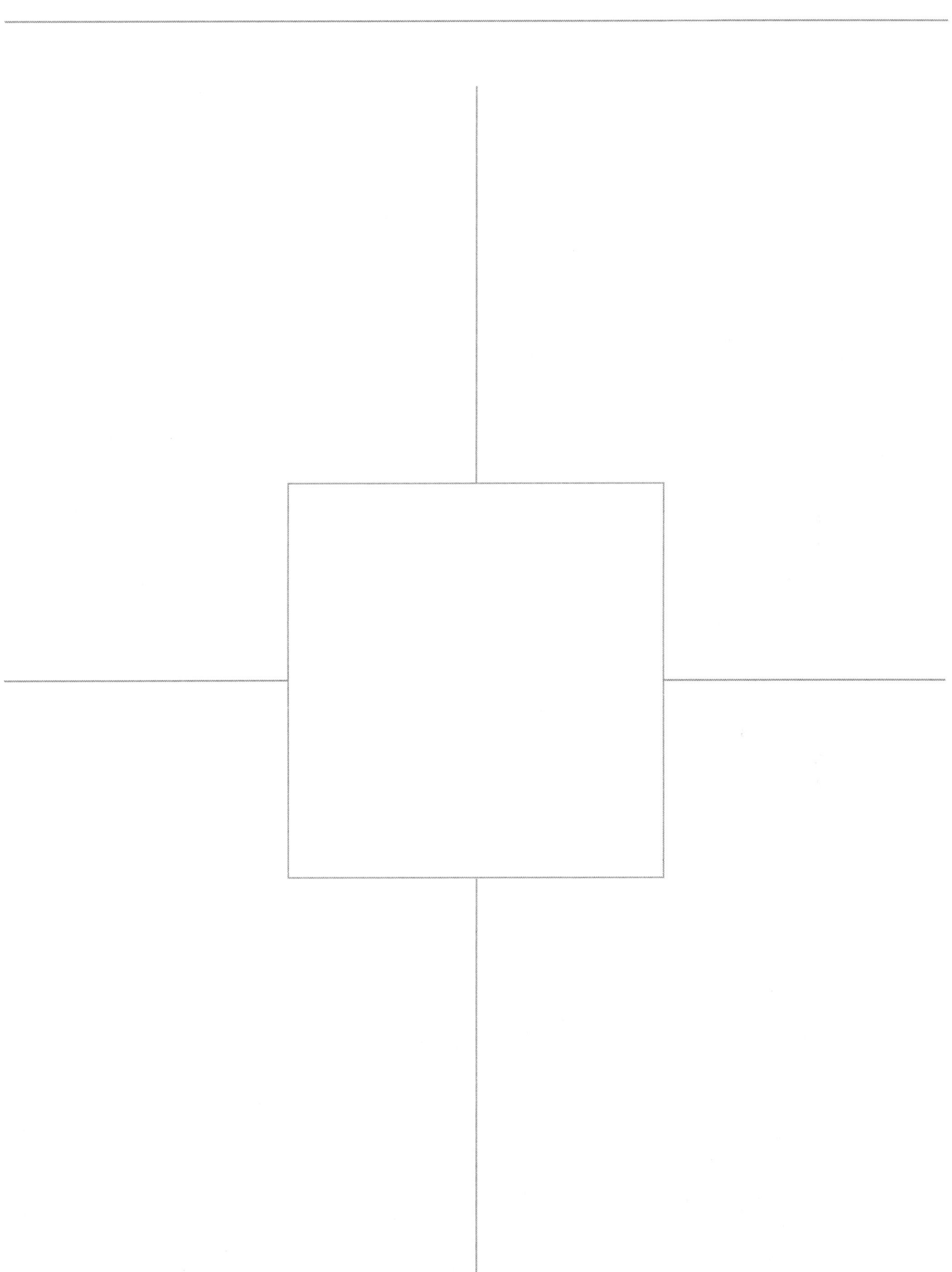

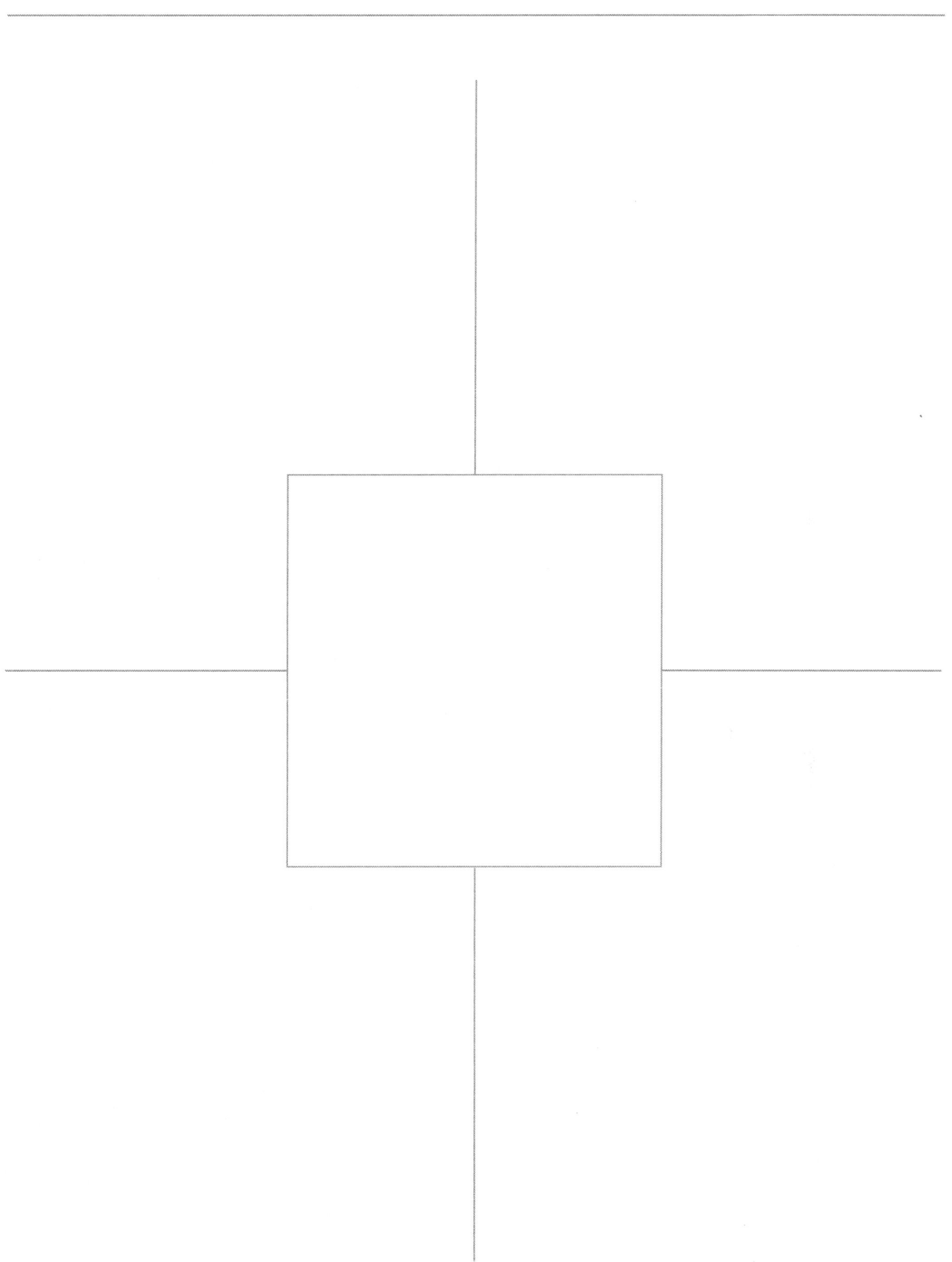

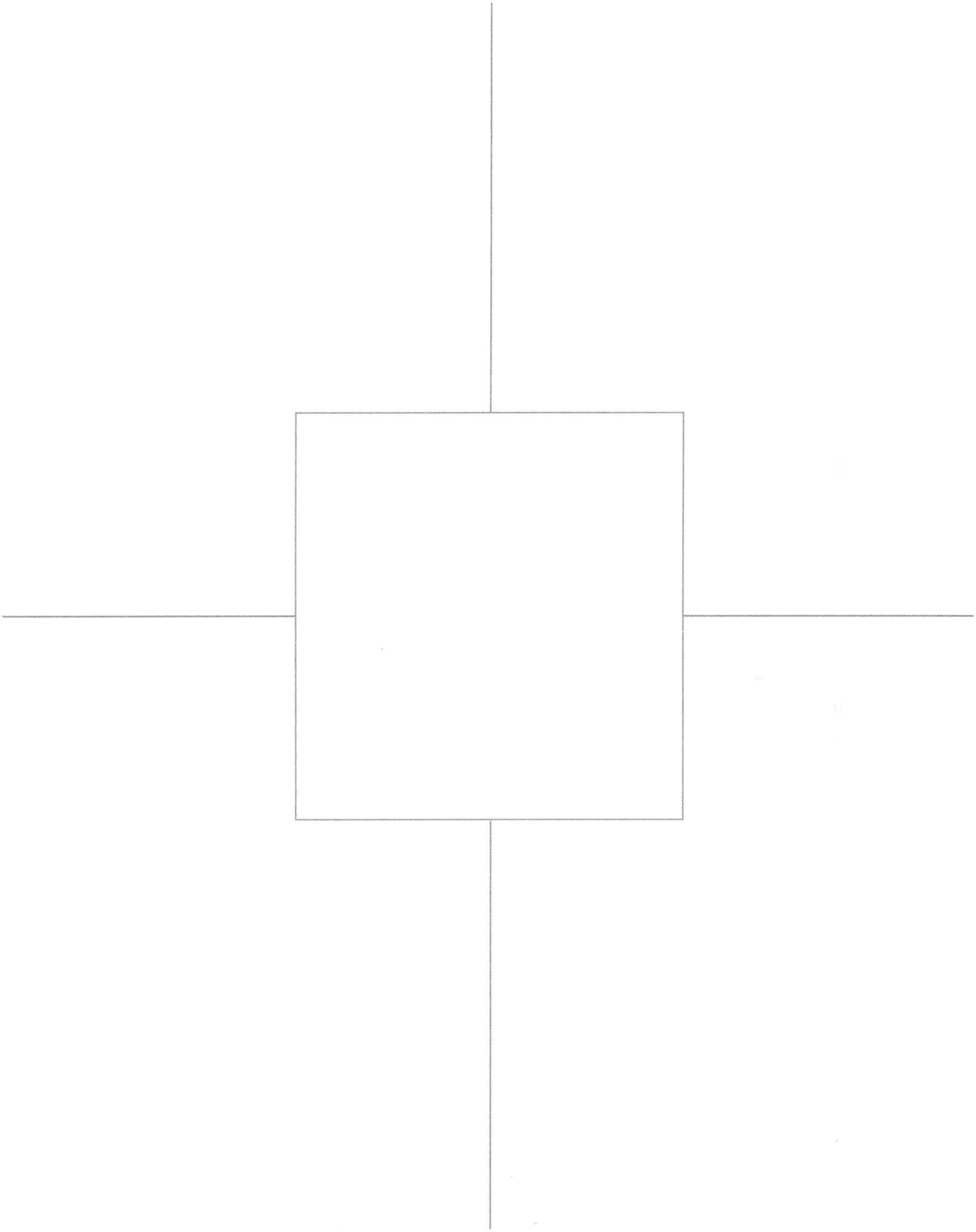

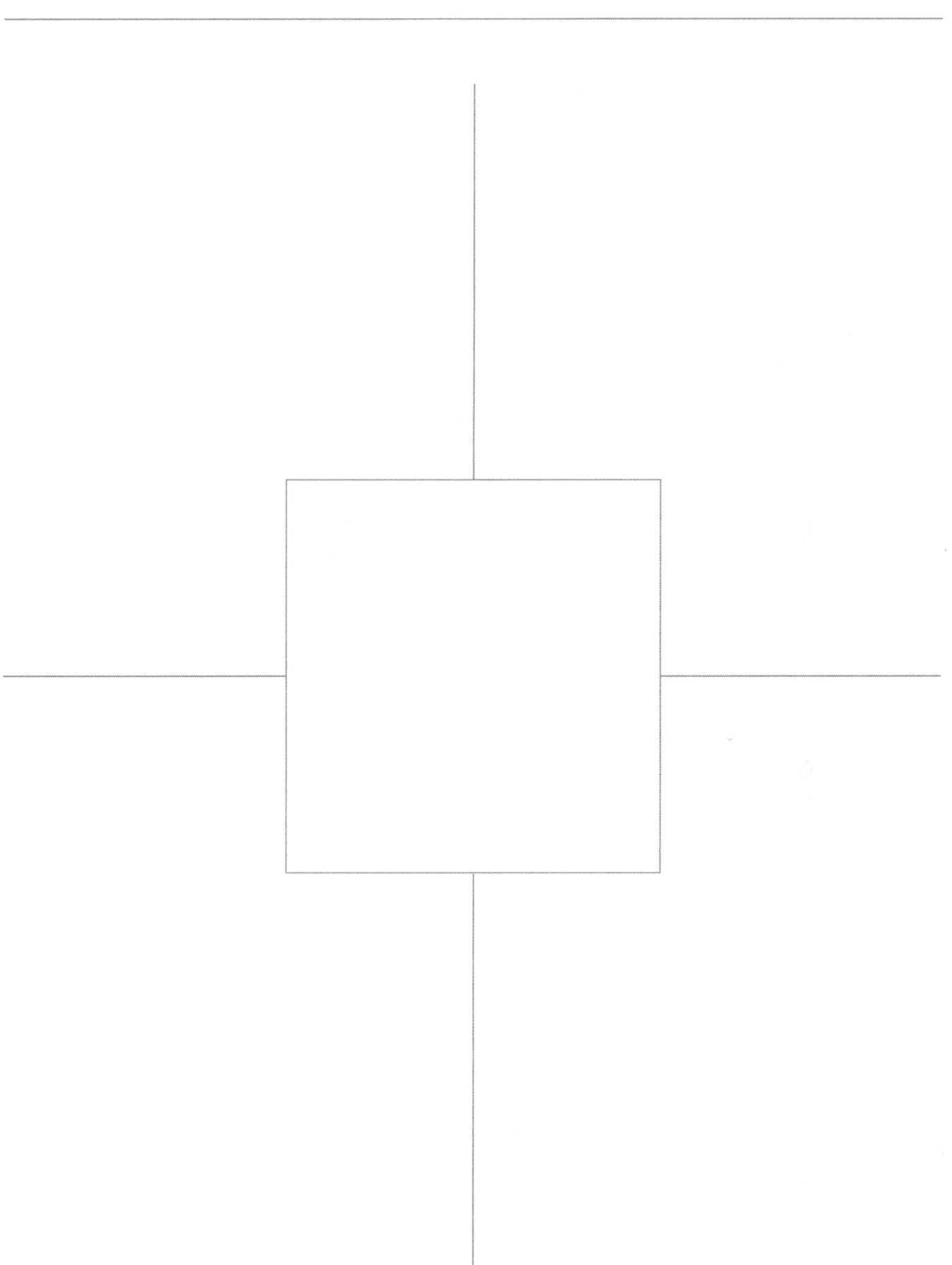

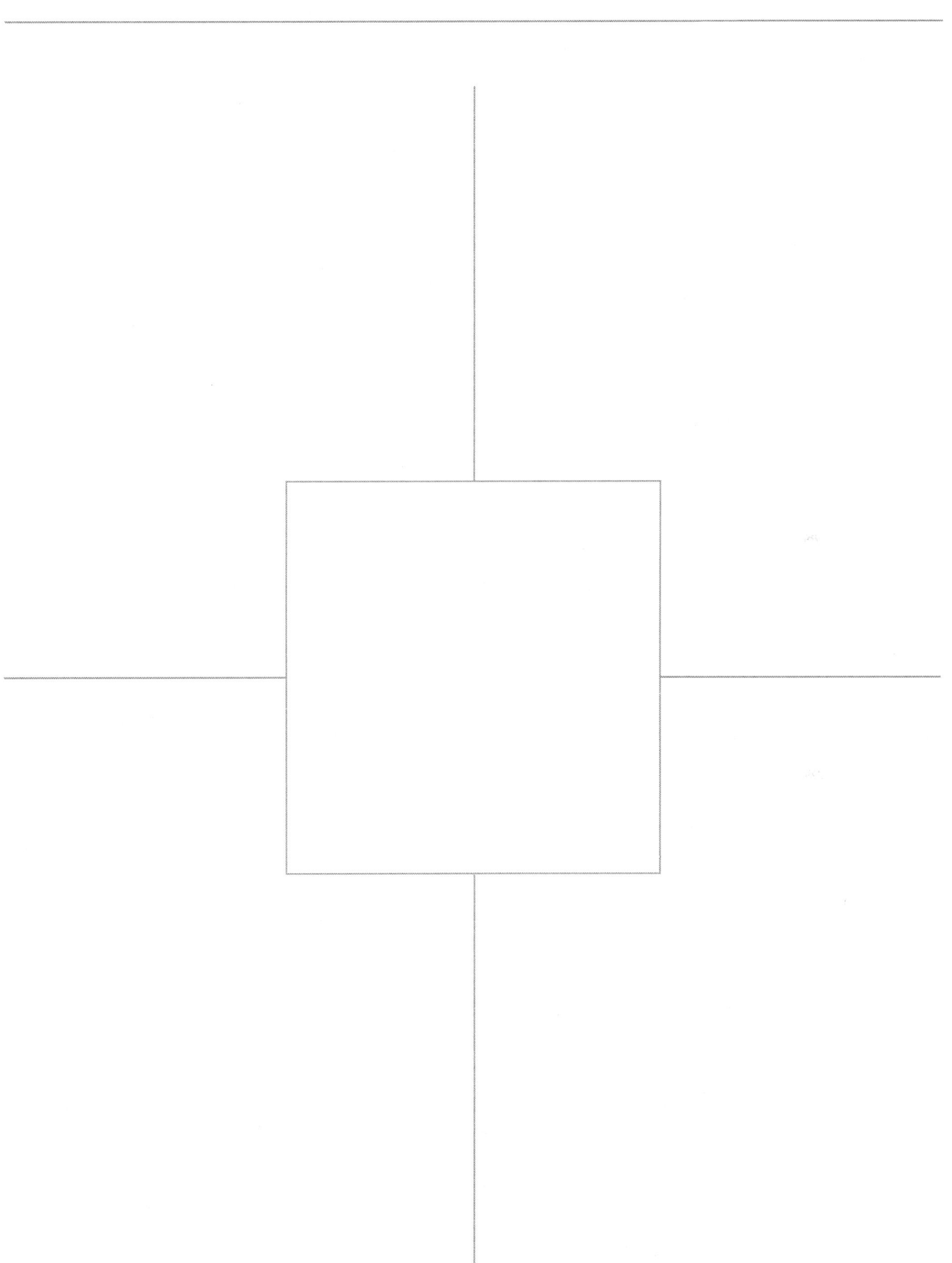

"Don't ask yourself what the world needs. Ask yourself what makes you come alive, and go do that, because what the world needs is people who have come alive."

–Howard Thurman
The Living Wisdom of Howard Thurman: A Visionary for Our Time

VOCATIONAL DISCERNMENT

Listening for and responding to God's call to ministry is a practice that undergirds our spiritual life. In *God's Plans for Us*, Brian Hall writes of discernment as the process of making choices through the eyes of faith so that we are brought closer to the person of Christ. It is perceiving God at work in everyday events and aligning our choices with this perception. What we are choosing are values, behaviors, and life-styles that bring us more into line with God's will for us.

Discernment looks to the objective facts of the situation and to the inner yearnings of the individual for clues as to where one is called. Because the Christian tradition teaches that God is revealed in history, our own stories and the stories of those around us can provide those clues. Discernment also requires us to listen to that still small voice within. Yes, we are subject to confusion and illusion, so we cannot do this task as isolated individuals; we need to test our sense of call with others and against Scripture and tradition.

Discernment is always provisional and must be tested by its fruits. Discernment is not a once-in-a-lifetime process. We need continually to assess whether or not our choices are in alignment and continue to fit within our growing faith and the situations of our everyday lives.

Responding to God's call is shaped by the regular practice of attention to personal and community contexts. What are the needs of the community around me? What gift can I offer? What implications for my own or others' action in ministry can be taken? What are the next steps? What or who will be needed to support me in this response?

Freedom is a prerequisite for discernment. When we close our hearts and minds and think we have all the answers, we are not ready for discerning the Spirit's urging. When we feel that there is only one way to do God's will, we are not ready to search freely for the interaction of our will with God's. Freedom for ministry means being free of both our fears and our attachments. It means "letting go."

As stated in Hebrews, "Faith is the assurance of things hoped for, the conviction of things not seen." It is trust in God's abiding presence. As our faith grows, we change and expand our convictions about what it is we ultimately trust. Faith involves making certain choices about the values which center our lives. Discernment requires that we discover the values that already empower and ground our ministry. In the process of discernment, we will discover our own values as we wrestle with the values that energized the life of Jesus.

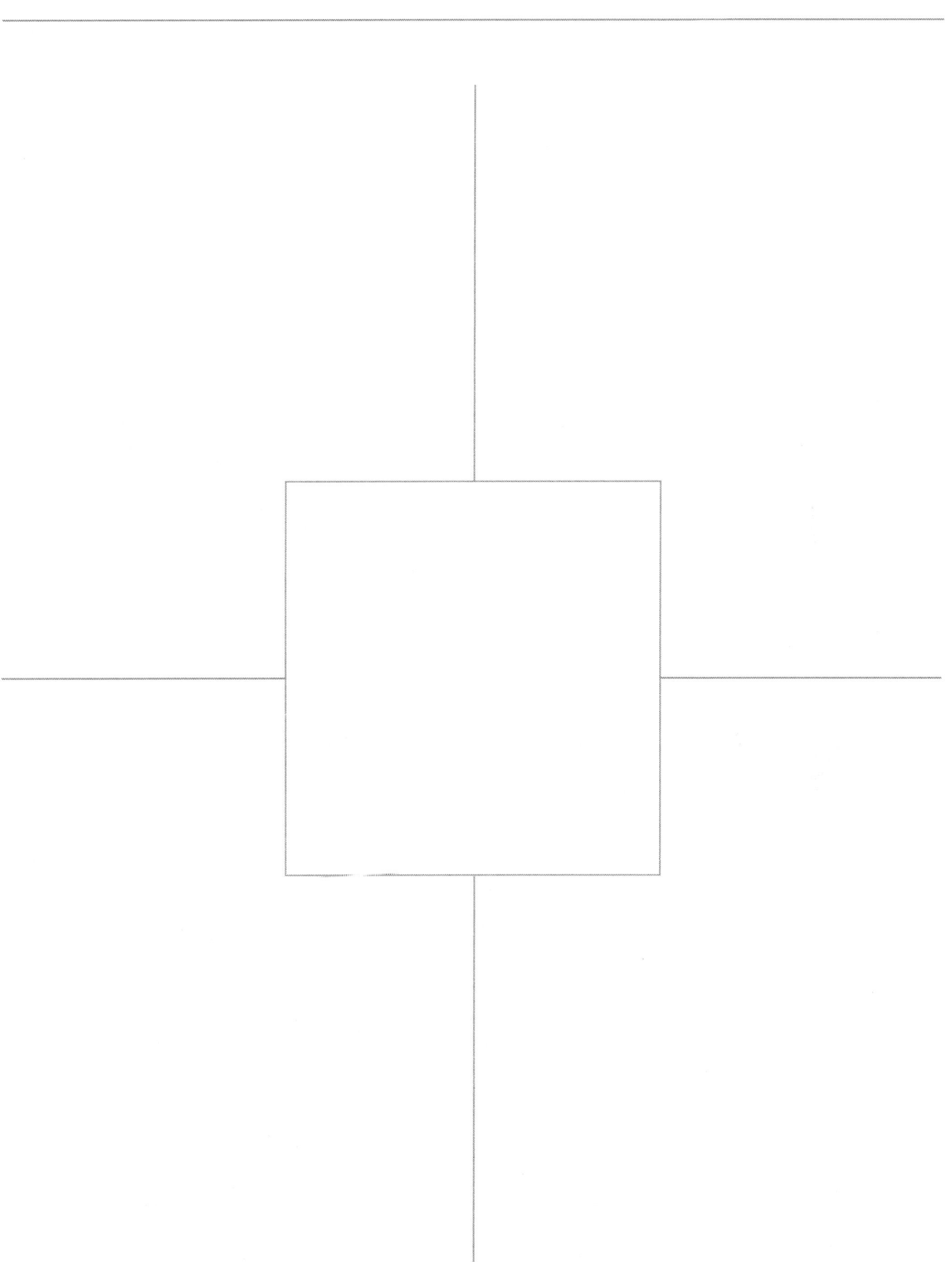

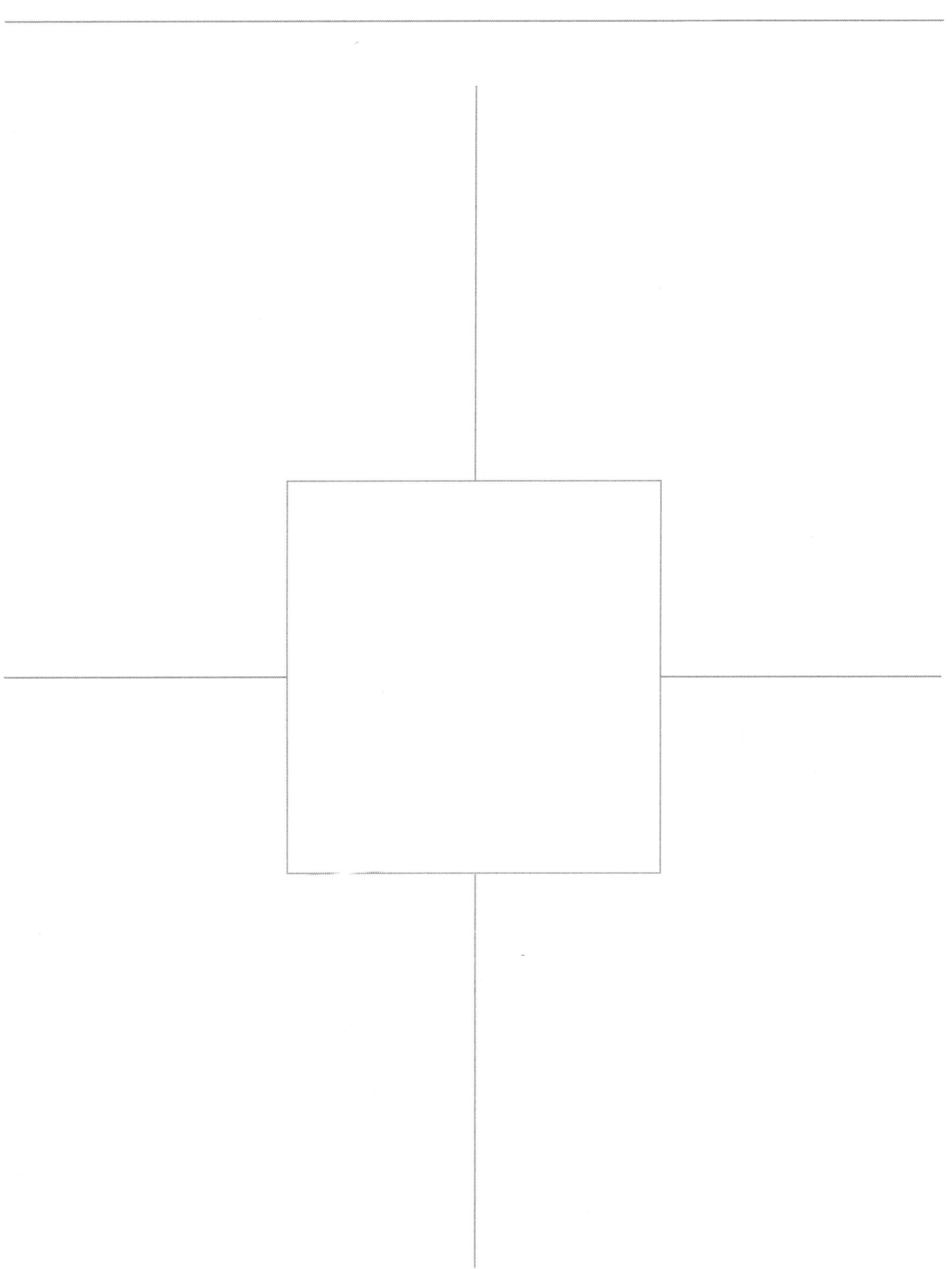

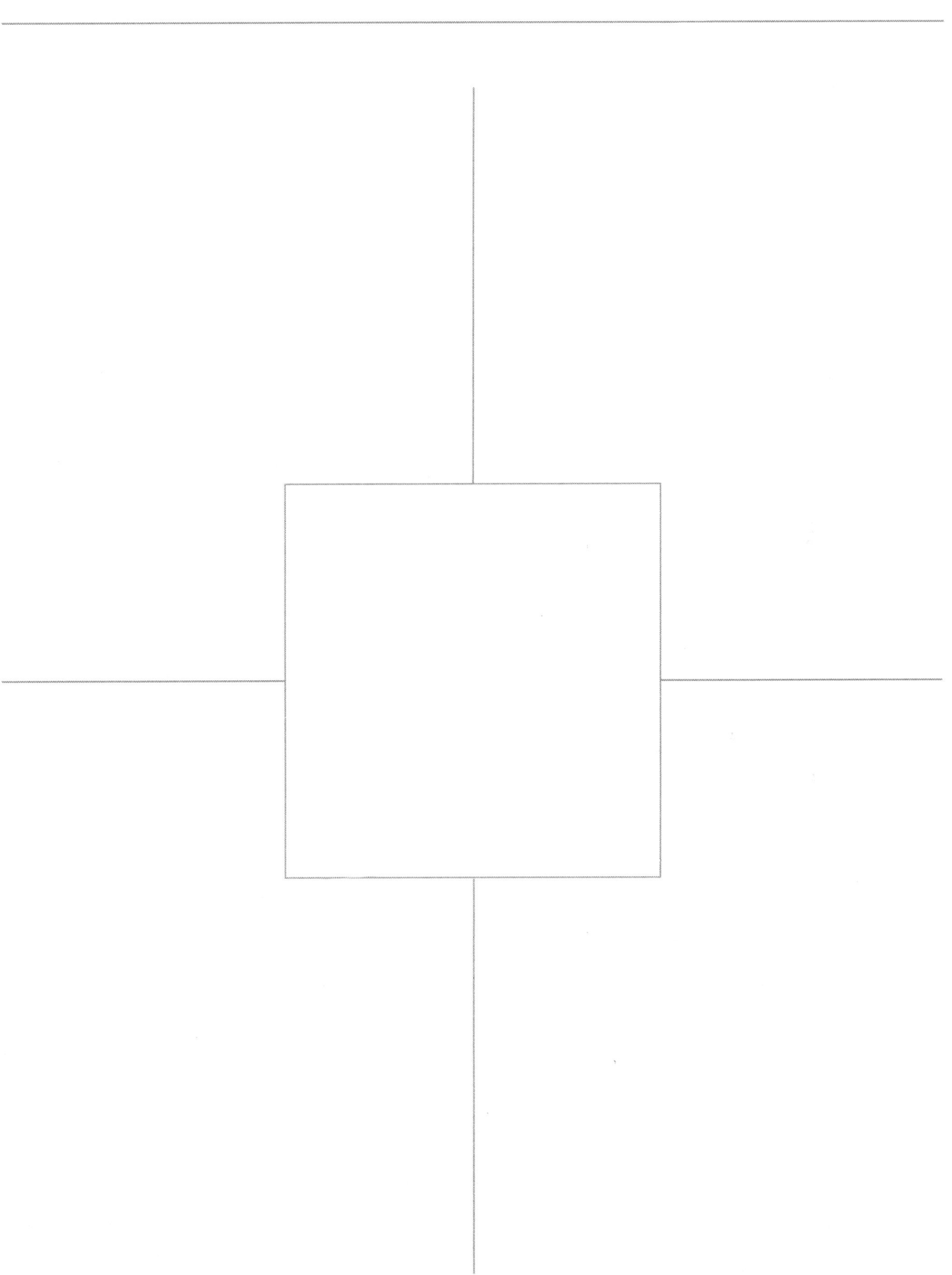

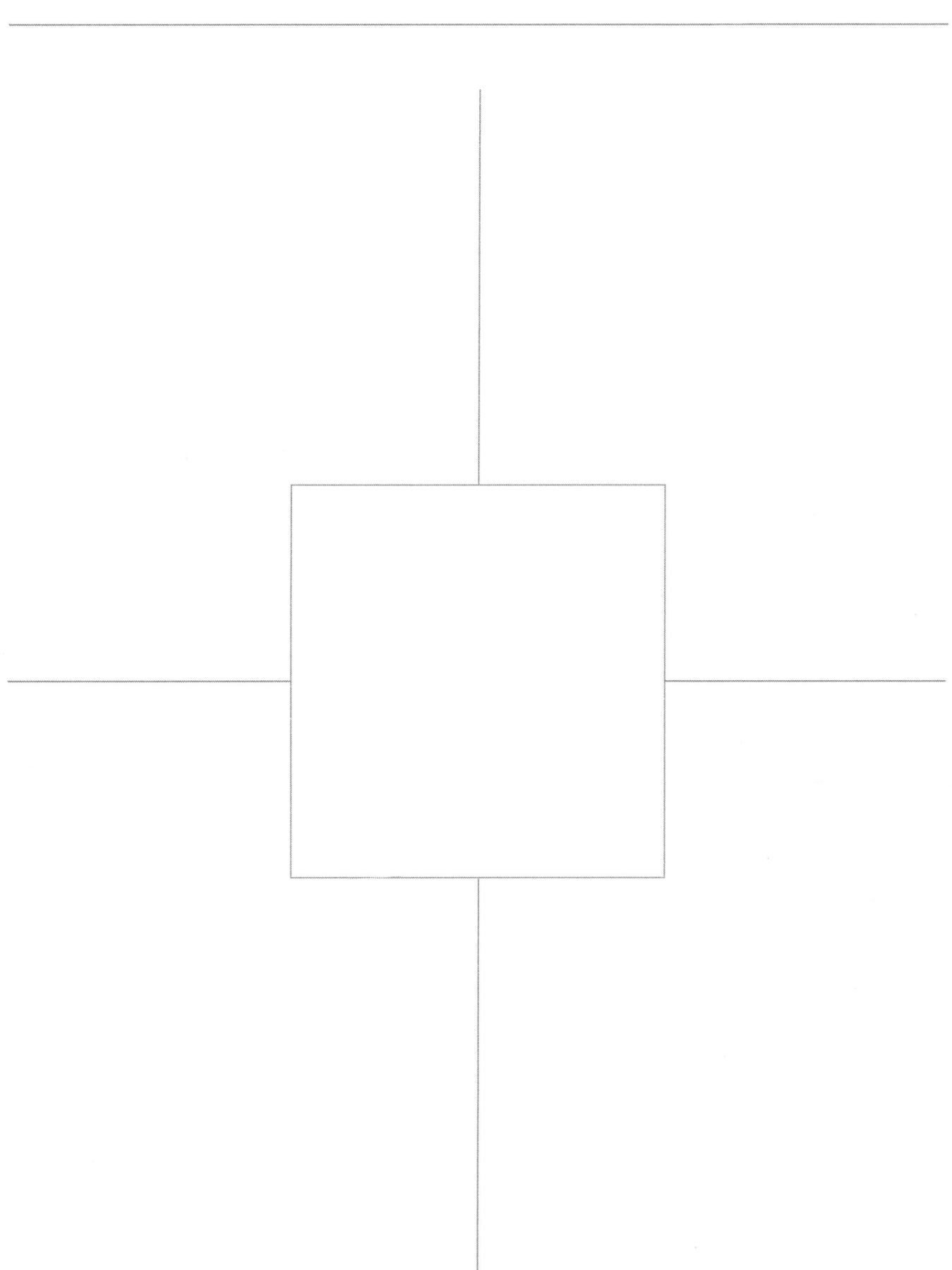

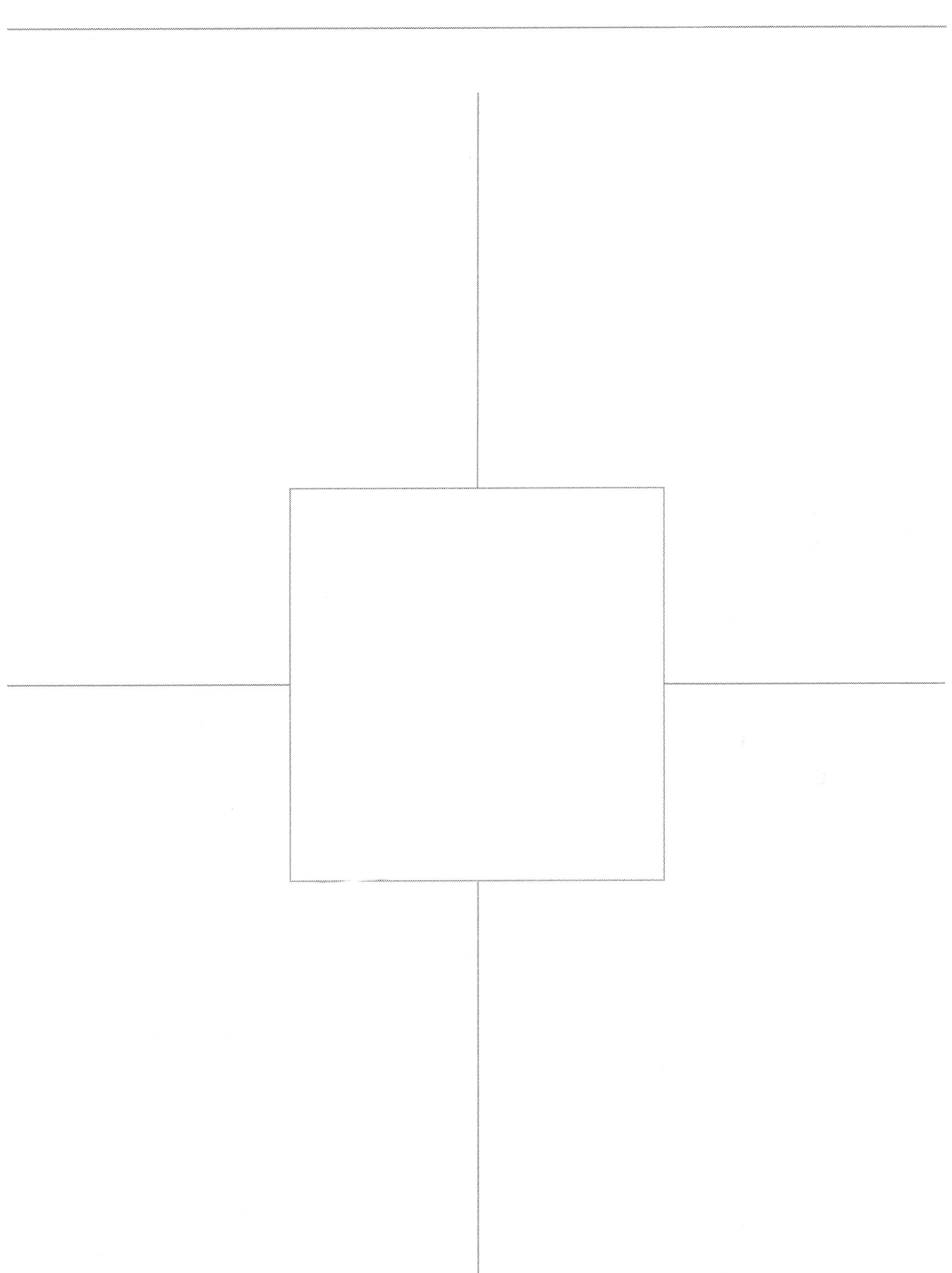

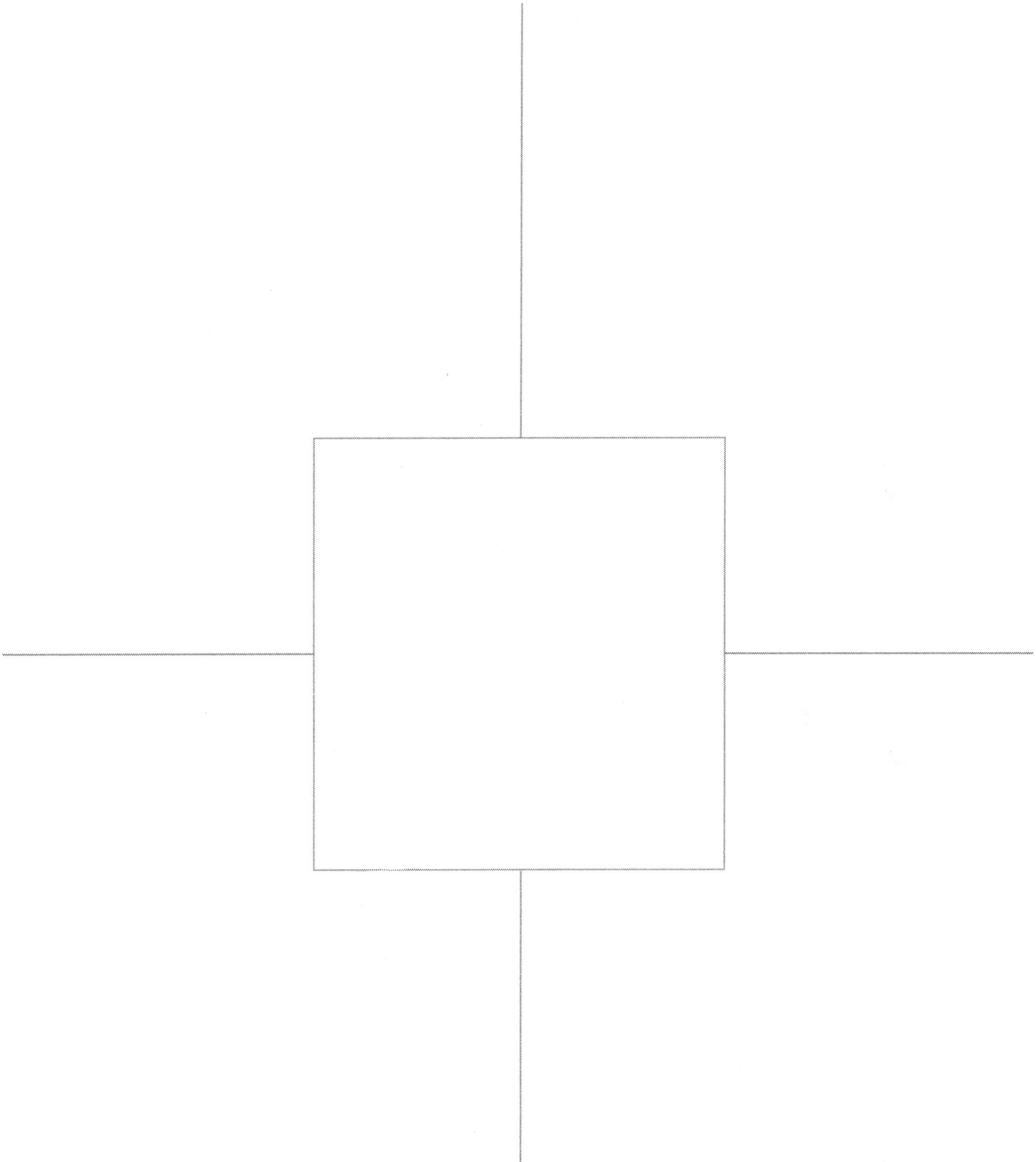

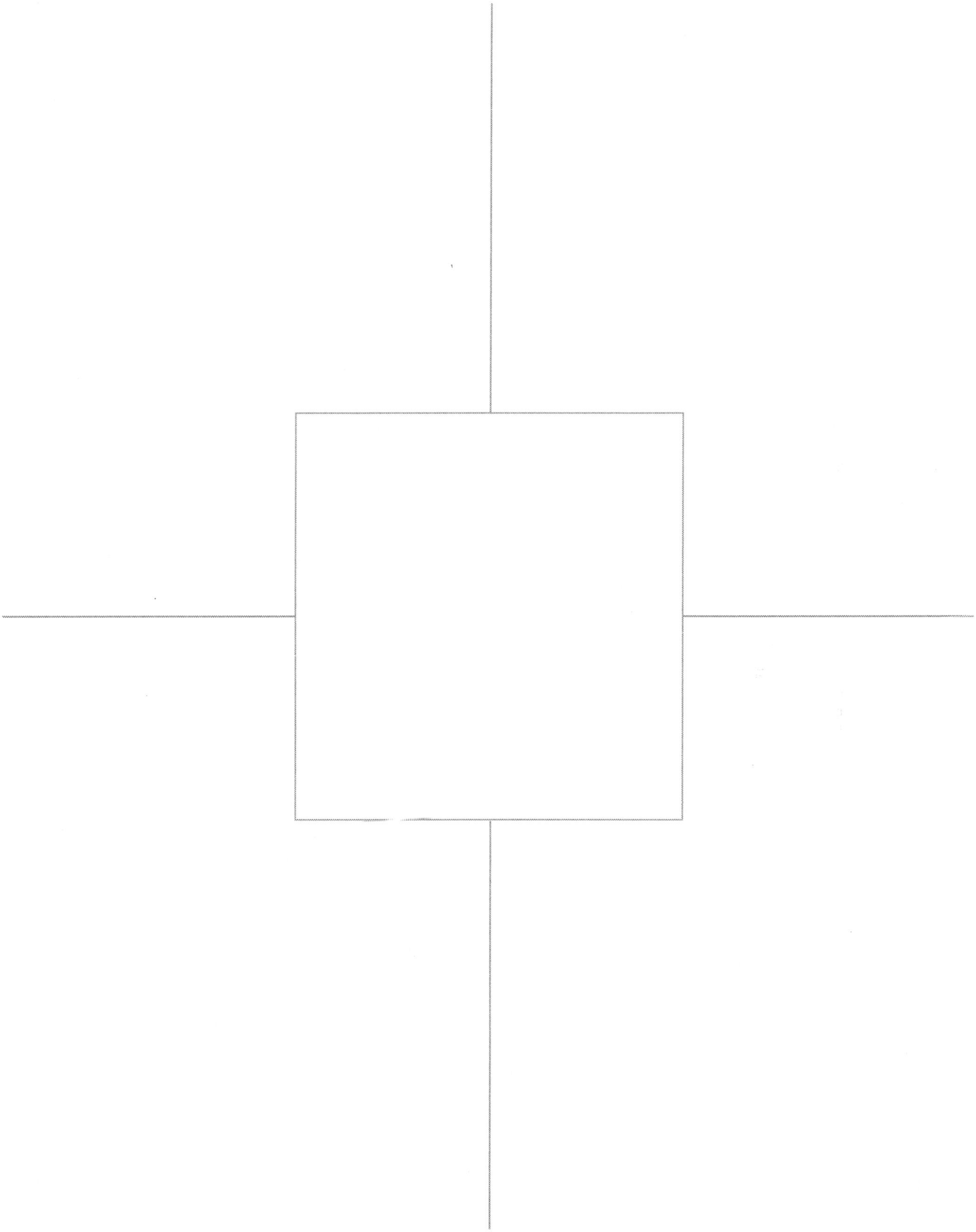

MINISTRY

One way to understand ministry is to see it as the participation with God realizing God's dream. Ministry happens among and within the complexities of the world. Clearly, contemporary life is complex and fast-paced, filled with multiple encounters with ethnic diversity. Education for Ministry brings people together by forming a reflecting community of colleagues committed to helping one another to know better what it means to live as an adult Christian in an increasingly pluralistic world.

Vocation, as understood from a United States cultural perspective, is a word that often refers to individual decisions that determine what income-producing activity a person wants to pursue. Young persons frequently are asked, "What do you want to be when you grow up?" Children recite rhymes that playfully indicate what the future may hold: "Rich man, poor man, beggar man, thief." These mirror cultural expectations that one day the child must hold a job taking on his or her vocation as an adult. On the other hand, the question, "Do you have a vocation?" is sometimes understood as decidedly religious. For much of history in the Christian tradition "having a vocation" meant becoming ordained or entering a religious order. From this perspective, those who "have" a vocation are said to be "called" to become clergy, monks, or nuns. Both meanings of "vocation" direct attention to how a person participates in society's institutional life.

Sociologists name five institutions, each needing people to lead, maintain, and develop them: religion, education, government, family, and economy. Religious institutions in North America are generally understood to mean congregations, but may include related institutions such as outreach centers and denominational offices (diocese or district). Non-Christians may use different terms, but all religious institutions need people to lead and maintain them. Government institutions that order society by providing laws and regulations need people to lead, maintain, and develop them as well; so, too, with economic, educational, and family institutions. Participation in any of the basic institutions can be designated as a vocation.

Vocation and ministry operate in concert with one another. In its most practical sense, vocation is expressed in ministry. Thus, vocational discernment is focused not only on whether one has a "call" but also on what one is being called to do. Further, a person's response to the discerned call draws on four formative factors. Shaping a ministry involves a view of self (identity). An individual ministers in a particular style or way of being in the situation that reflects an orientation to daily life (attitude). Basic concepts, narratives, images, and information contribute to understanding (knowledge). As one takes action, the ability to act effectively and efficiently comes into play (skill). The identity, attitude, knowledge, and skill of the minister contribute to any expression of vocation in ministry.

A ministry is fashioned through a dynamic process of decision, commitment, discipline, experience, and reflection. Decisions made contribute to commitment. Discipline in carrying out the commitment in action with skill and grace develops patterns of experience. Cumulative experience enriches action as one reflects on learning in the dynamic process. The process continues with each compelling sense to take action, in other words, with each discernment of vocation. A coherent theology of vocation, expressed in ministry, is understood as contributing to God's purpose and the vision provides motivating energy and animates ministry within individuals and institutions.

Finally, as the expression of vocation through ministry is identified and takes shape, the question of sustainability should be part of the discourse. Because we live in a dynamic, fluid world in which change is a constant reality, vocational decisions may be formed with a sense of impermanence. The image of maneuvering in permanent white water aptly describes present realities, whether viewed from individual, institutional, or global levels, raising questions of sustainability, relevance, and flourishing. "Can the direction of my life be sustained and for how long?" "What relevance does my individual life and the institutions in which I work have for the big picture?" "What keeps my ministry fresh and vibrant?" Questions concerning sustaining and flourishing are central to theological positioning and need to be considered in creating a mature and comprehensive vocational theology.

"Christians are usually sincere and well-intentioned people until you get to any real issues of ego, control power, money, pleasure, and security. Then they tend to be pretty much like everybody else. We are often given a bogus version of the Gospel, some fast-food religion, without any deep transformation of the self; and the result has been the spiritual disaster of "Christian" countries that tend to be as consumer-oriented, proud, warlike, racist, class conscious, and addictive as everybody else-and often more so, I'm afraid."

–Richard Rohr
Breathing Underwater: Spirituality and the 12 Steps

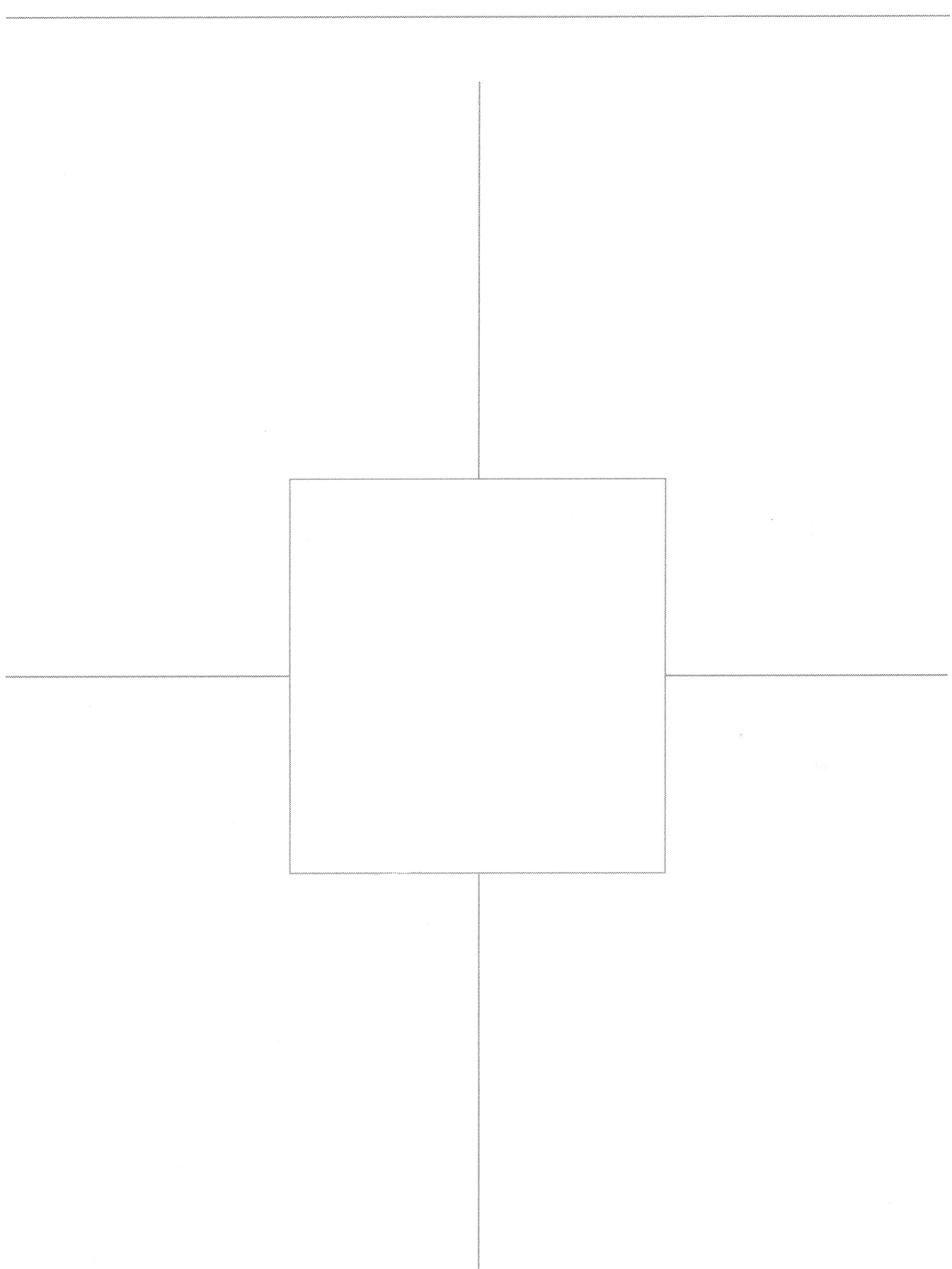

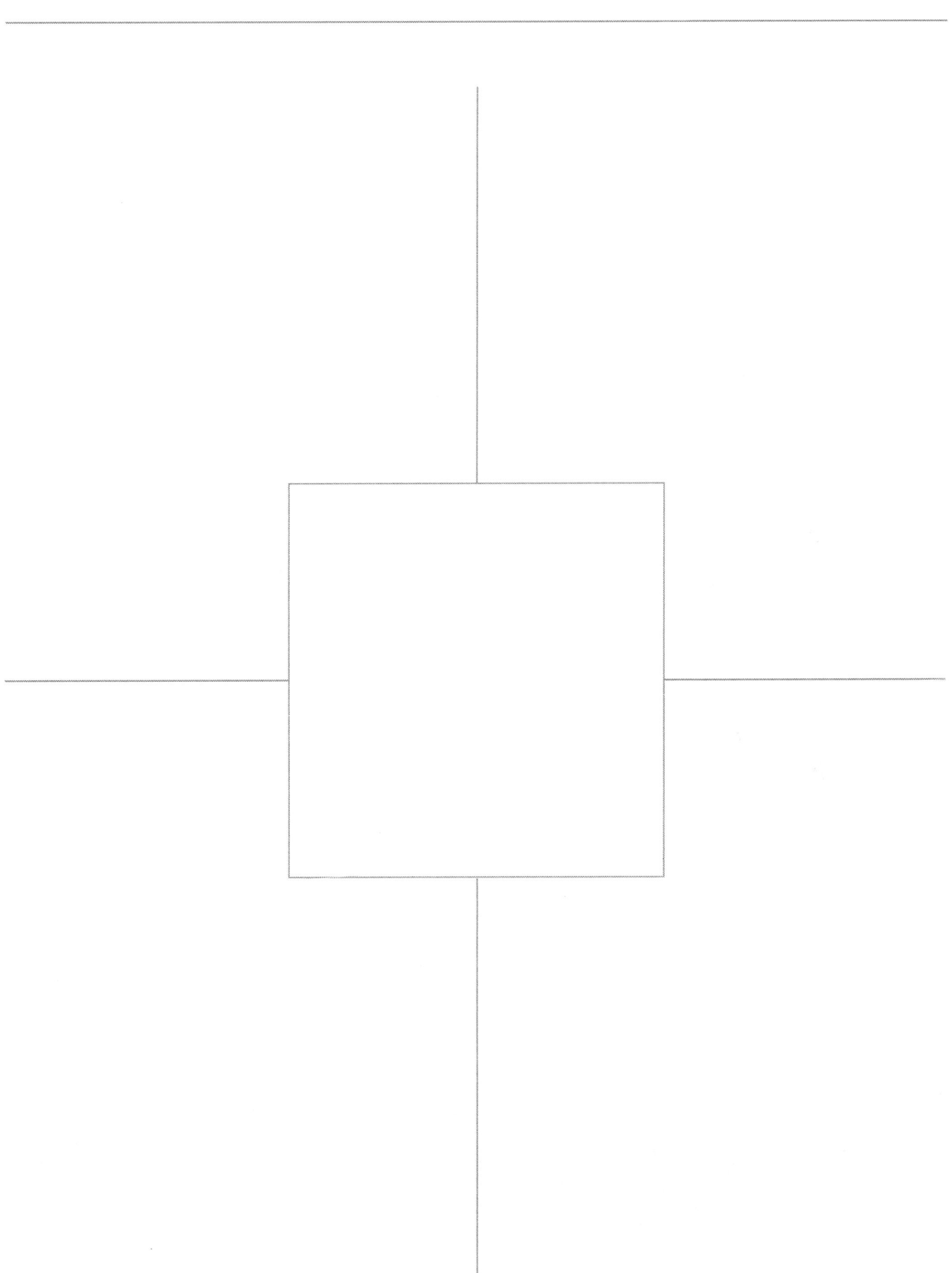

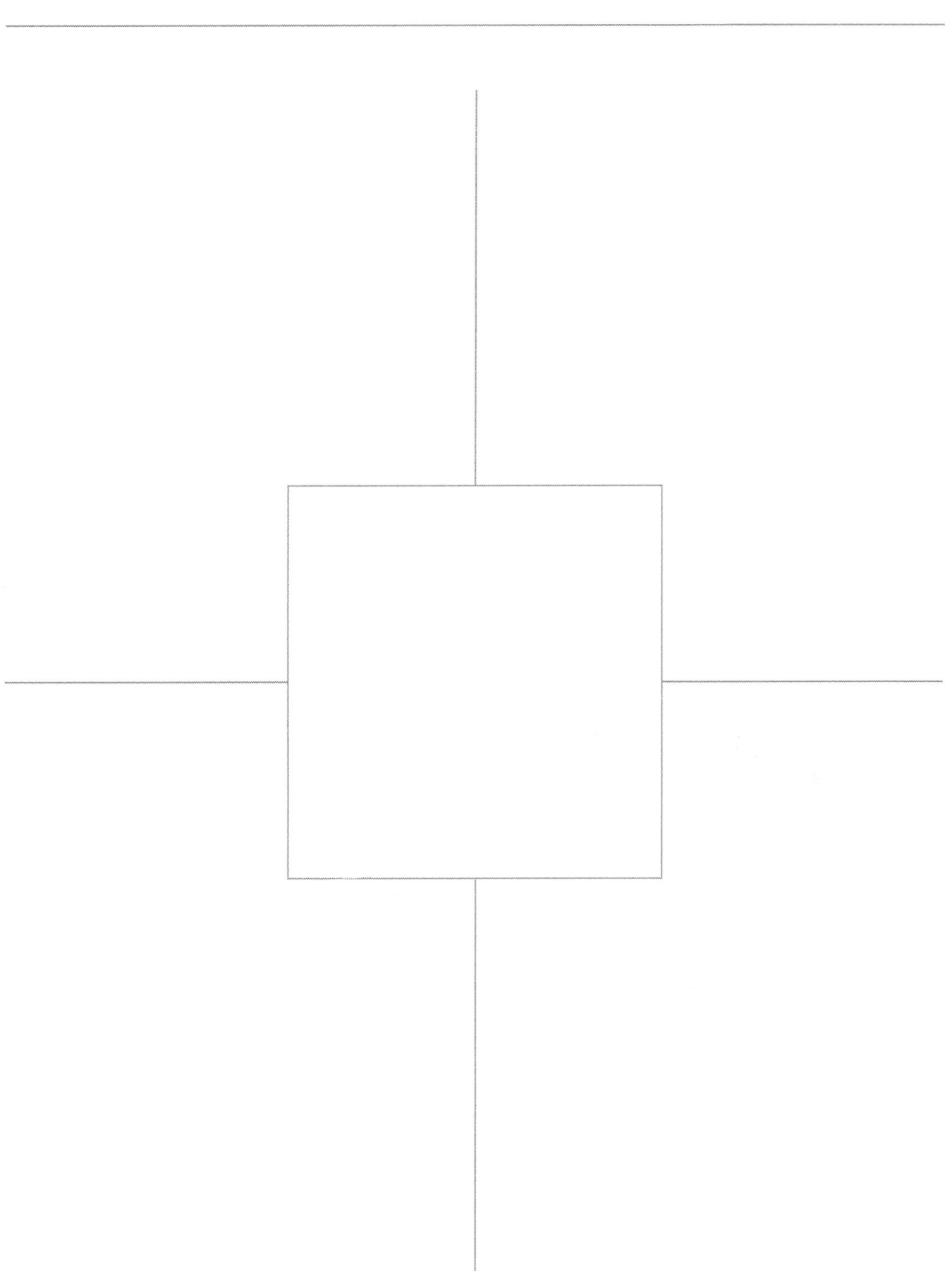

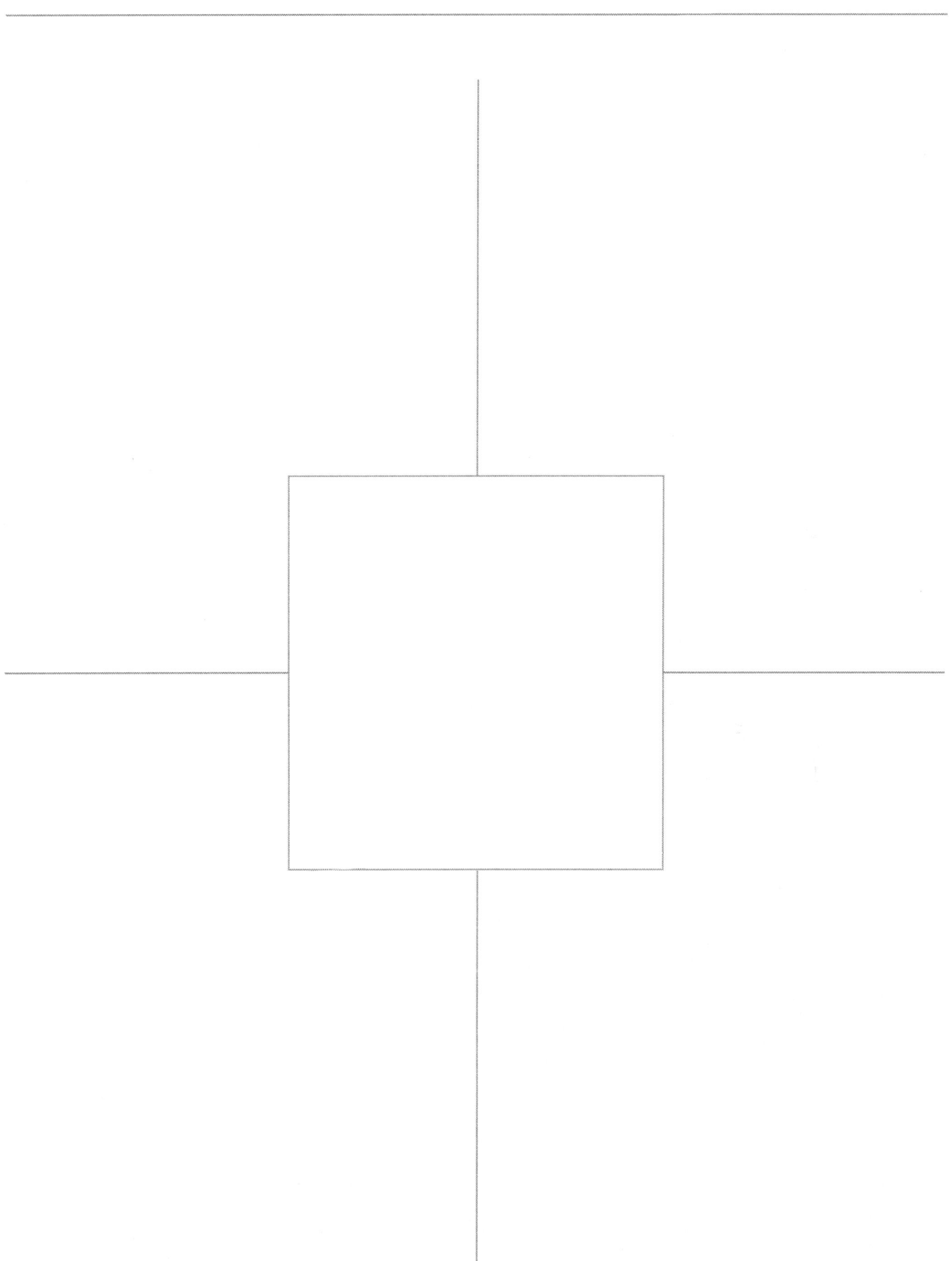

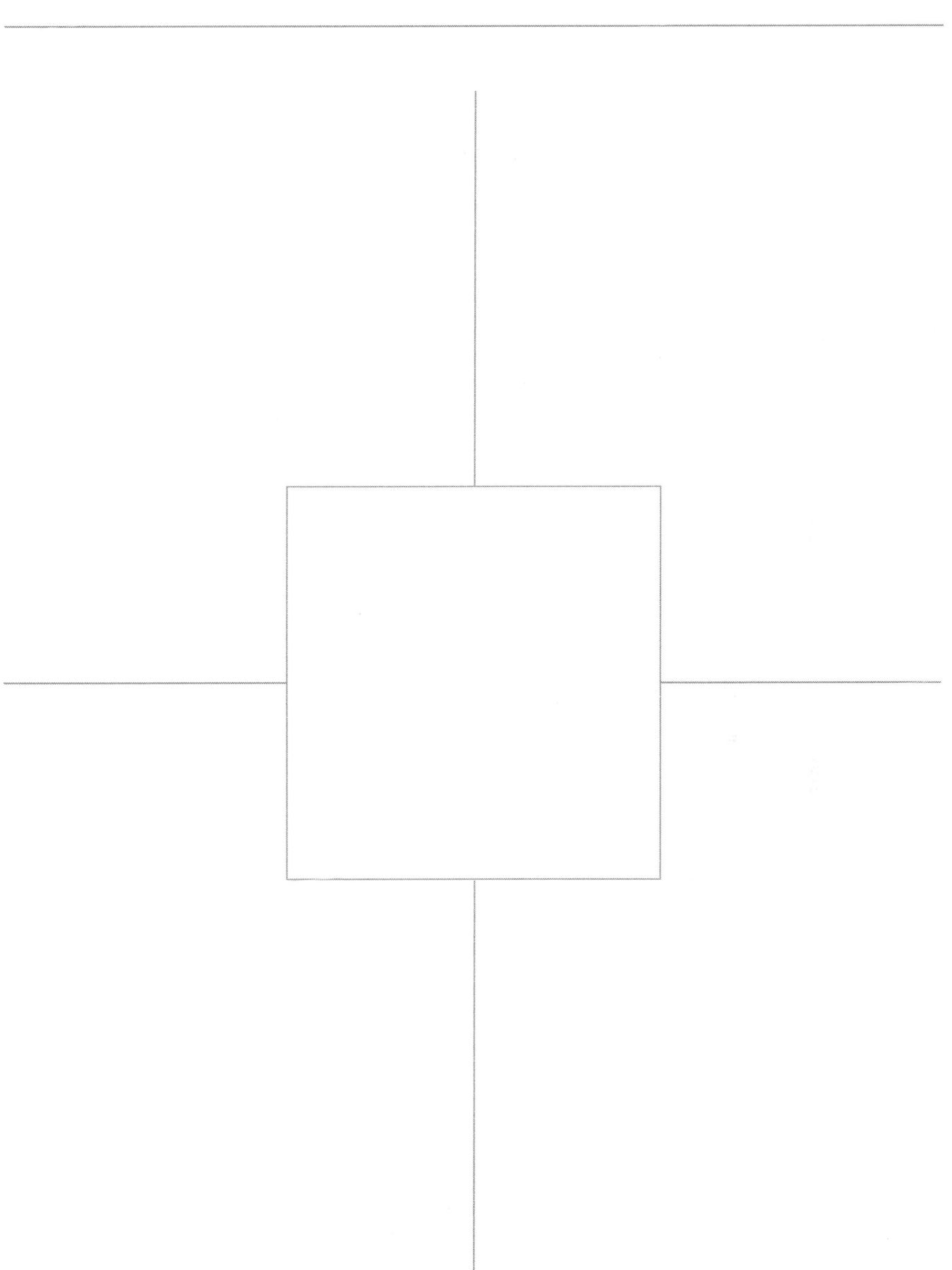

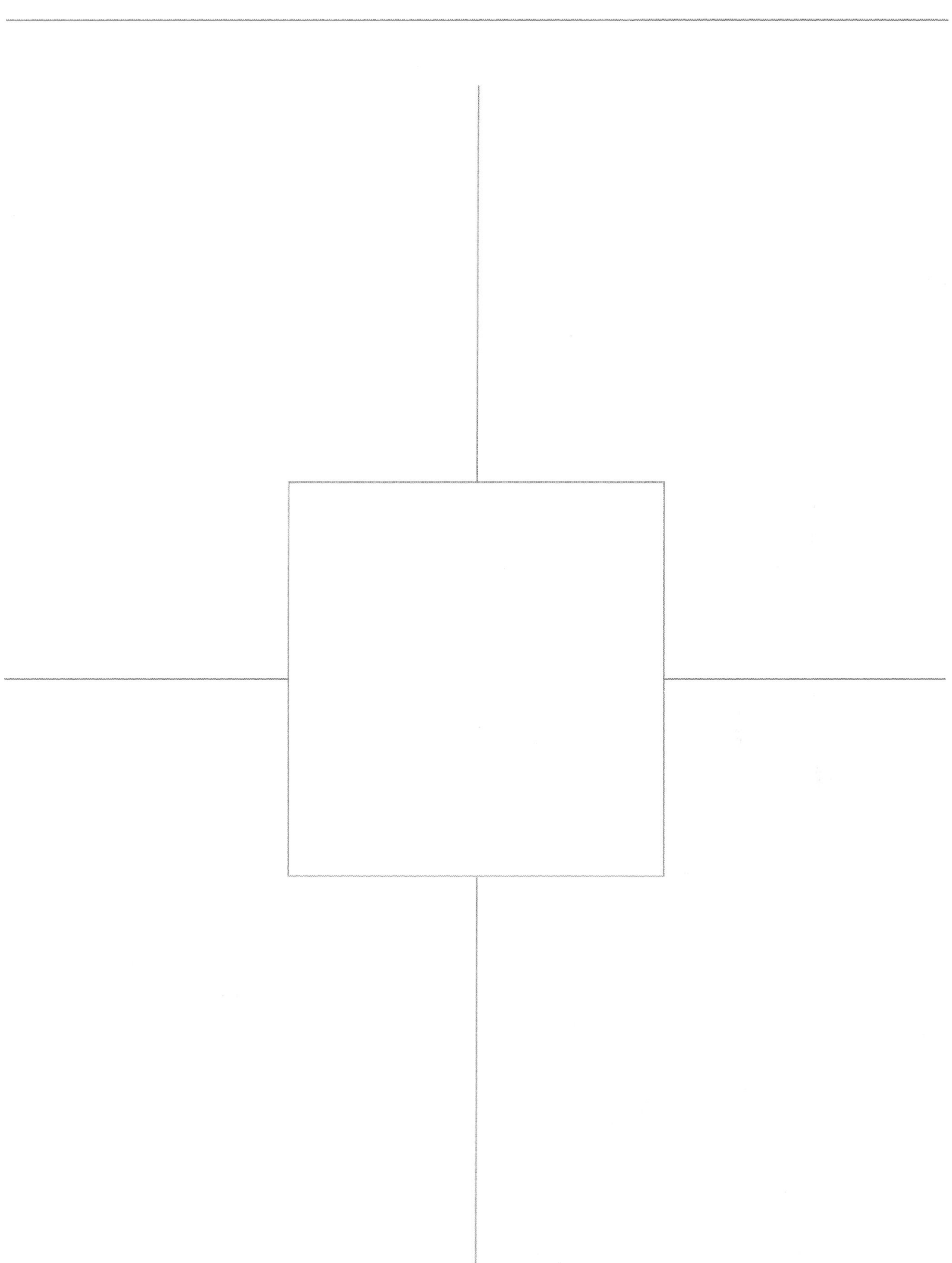

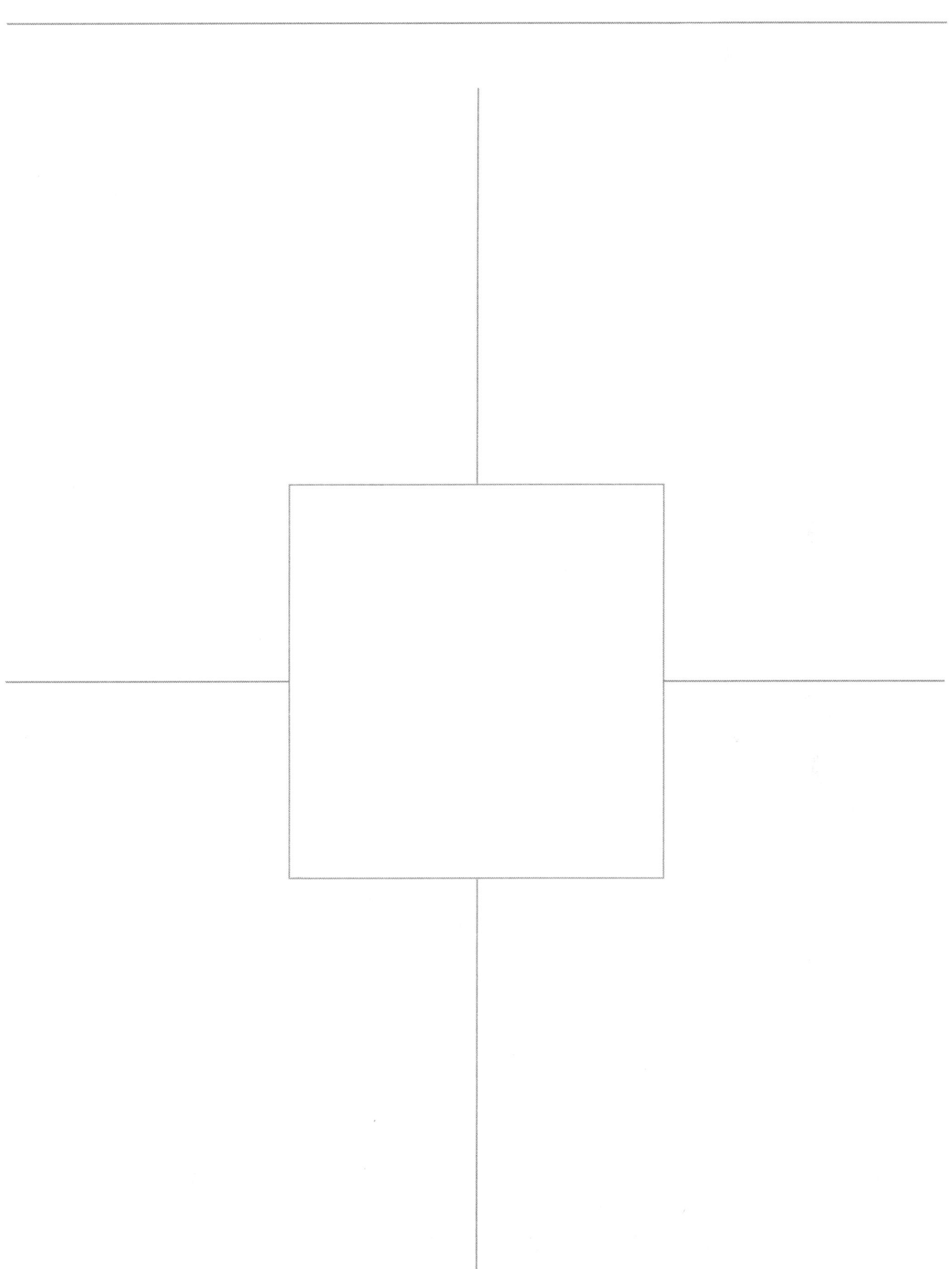

STEPPING STONES

In EfM, we begin to reflect upon our own lives using a method called Stepping Stones. In the 1950s, Ira Progoff began studying human research as it relates to spiritual and physical growth. Originally, his work began at Drew University, a Methodist college located in New Jersey. There his research on creative persons led to the development of an extensive method for encouraging individual growth. Progroff says, "Each person is engaged in finding the way of life and of being that is true to our own nature."

As we begin to compose our spiritual autobiographies, how we find our path differs from others and may change as we grow and gain experience. The process of Stepping Stones for spiritual autobiography is based on several procedures Progoff developed for setting the context of one's life. For further information concerning his method, you can consult his book, At a Journal Workshop.

The image of walking along a stone path while reflecting on the direction of your life is a recurring theme in prayer. You might view each of these stones as stages in your life or simply as the passage of time. Putting things in order is important to do throughout our faith journey. Just as we use a compass, the sun, or the stars as a guide on a physical journey, we can recognize the connection between walking a path and one's faith as one deeply embedded in Christian culture.

In writing a spiritual autobiography, a stepping stone is something we recall as we consider our lives as a whole or in part. It is a word or a brief phrase that marks a period of our individual lives such as kids in diapers, early retirement, or an experience that stands out. Limiting the number of stepping stones to 10 or 12 is a good idea as you try to organize your thoughts. In this way, you can walk more easily through the flow of your entire life. Again, the purpose of the listing is for you to see the continuous movement of your life as a whole story.

You may begin by thinking about the question, "Where am I now in my life?" Write a few sentences that describe the general tone of atmosphere of this present period in your life. Consider what events mark it off. How far back into the past does it reach? What are the main characteristics of this recent time?

Next, expand your description by considering some specific content. Who are the people of special importance to you in this present period? How would you describe your relationship with them?

What are the work projects and activities that you find engaging? What are your physical conditions during this period? Comment on your health, your sensory life, your overall relationship to your body and its use during this period.

What are the social attitudes during this time, your beliefs, your loyalties? Describe your relation to your family, your nation, your social roots.

Who are the persons who have inspired you?

Once you have a description of your perception of your present situation you are ready to examine the context of your life as a whole. Progoff's stepping stone technique allows us to reflect upon the events that come to our minds when we spontaneously reflect on the course that our lives may have taken from the beginning to the present moment. Identify a few stepping stones that help you get a sense of the flow of your life. What are its ups and downs, the quiet periods as well as the active times? Where was God? How was your spiritual health?

At some point you will have a fairly complete description of the stepping stones of your life. You may want to describe or delve more deeply into stones that grab your attention. Our spiritual life and history form a tapestry of our lives that may be seen in discrete section, but which really weave together into the greater tapestry of history. We are at once in history and apart from it.

Each person has a history because of their experiences. But not until the person's history is expressed does it have life. The telling generates the story, giving it form and meaning. Once expressed, a person's history becomes concrete and actual. It becomes something that can speak to the self.

"At the surface of our life we are conscious of the many pressing problems that beset us, the conflicts, the anxieties, the angers, the decisions that we feel we must urgently make. But one reason that the Intensive Journal method has been effective for many people is that it practices an indirect approach to slowing our life problems. Rather than move head-on to encounter problems in the external form in which they appear in our lives, we step back and move inward to meet them at a deeper level."

–Ira Progoff
At a Journal Workshop: Writing to Access the Power of the Unconscious and Evoke Creative Ability

Made in the USA
Columbia, SC
21 September 2025

afc76b27-e6de-408c-88f7-c1f8c58332b2R01